I DRAW FASHION

DIAMOND
FACE SHAPE

MAKEUP FACE CHARTS
FOR MAKEUP ARTISTS

MODEL: BLACK

CONTENTS

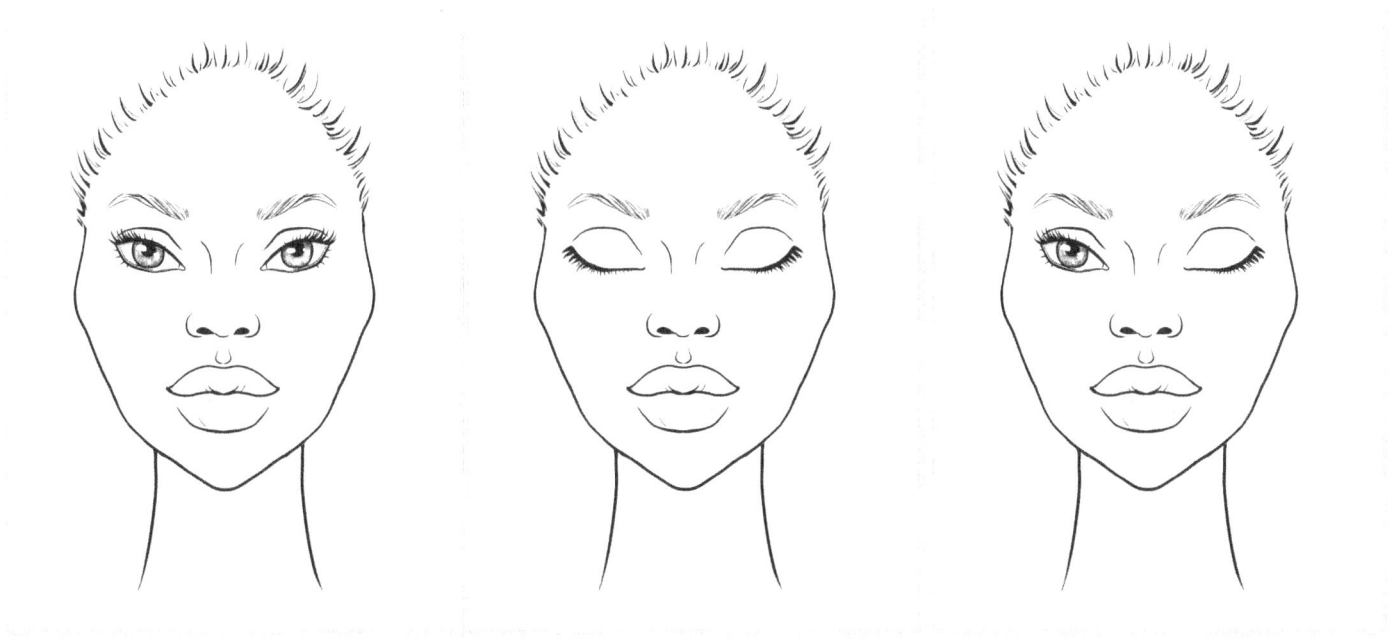

OPENED EYES
FACE CHARTS

PREPARATION

Cleanser

Moisturizer

Primer

FACE

Concealer

Foundation

Powder

Highlighter

Contour

Bronzer

Blush

EYES

Eyeshadow lid

Eyeshadow crease

Eyeliner

Mascara

Lashes

Brows

LIPS

Lip color

Lip liner

Lip gloss

OTHER

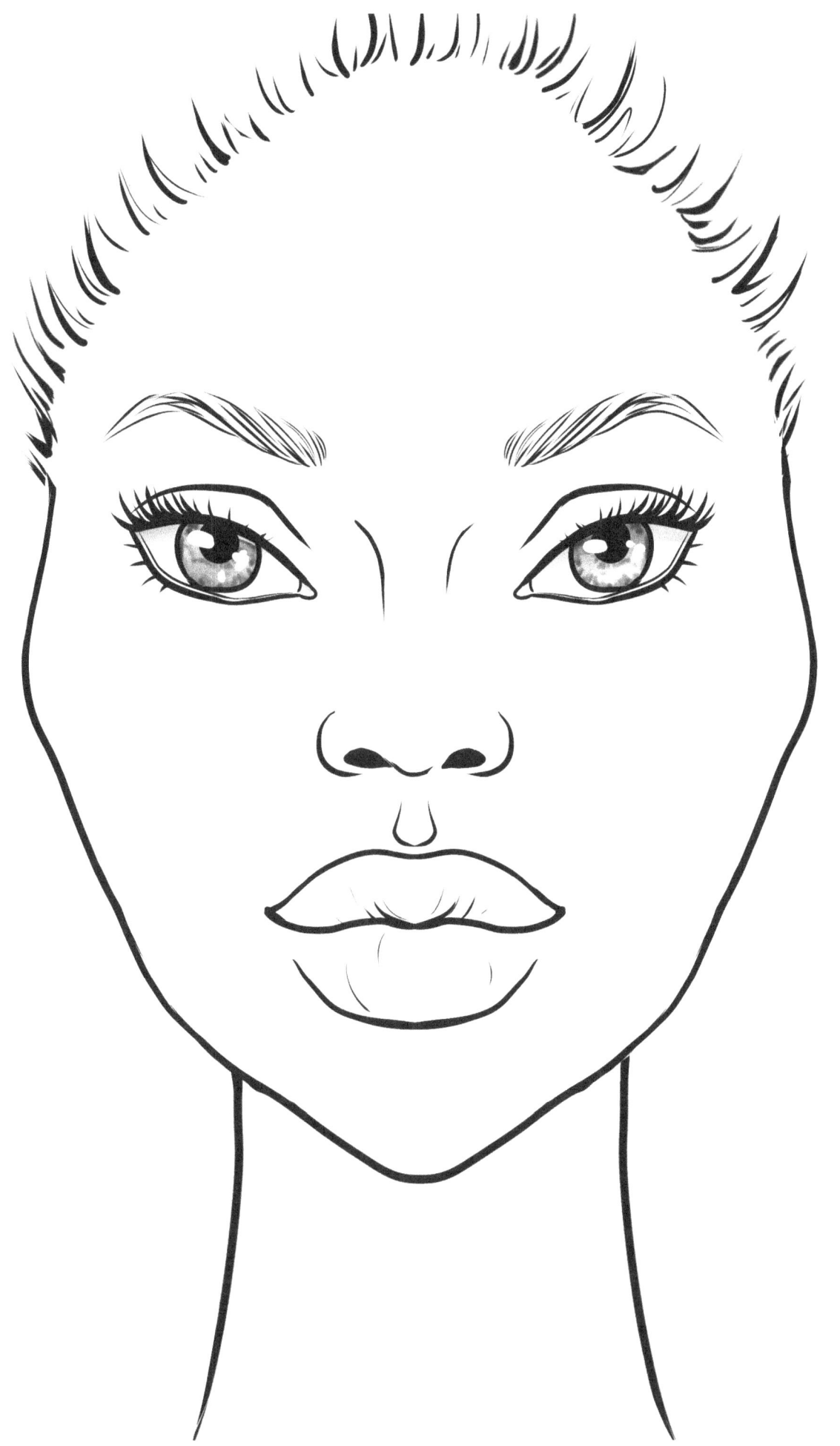

PREPARATION

Cleanser

_____

Moisturizer

_____

Primer

_____

FACE

Concealer

_____

Foundation

_____

Powder

_____

Highlighter

_____

Contour

_____

Bronzer

_____

Blush

_____

EYES

Eyeshadow lid

_____

Eyeshadow crease

_____

Eyeliner

_____

Mascara

_____

Lashes

_____

Brows

_____

LIPS

Lip color

_____

Lip liner

_____

Lip gloss

_____

OTHER

_____

_____

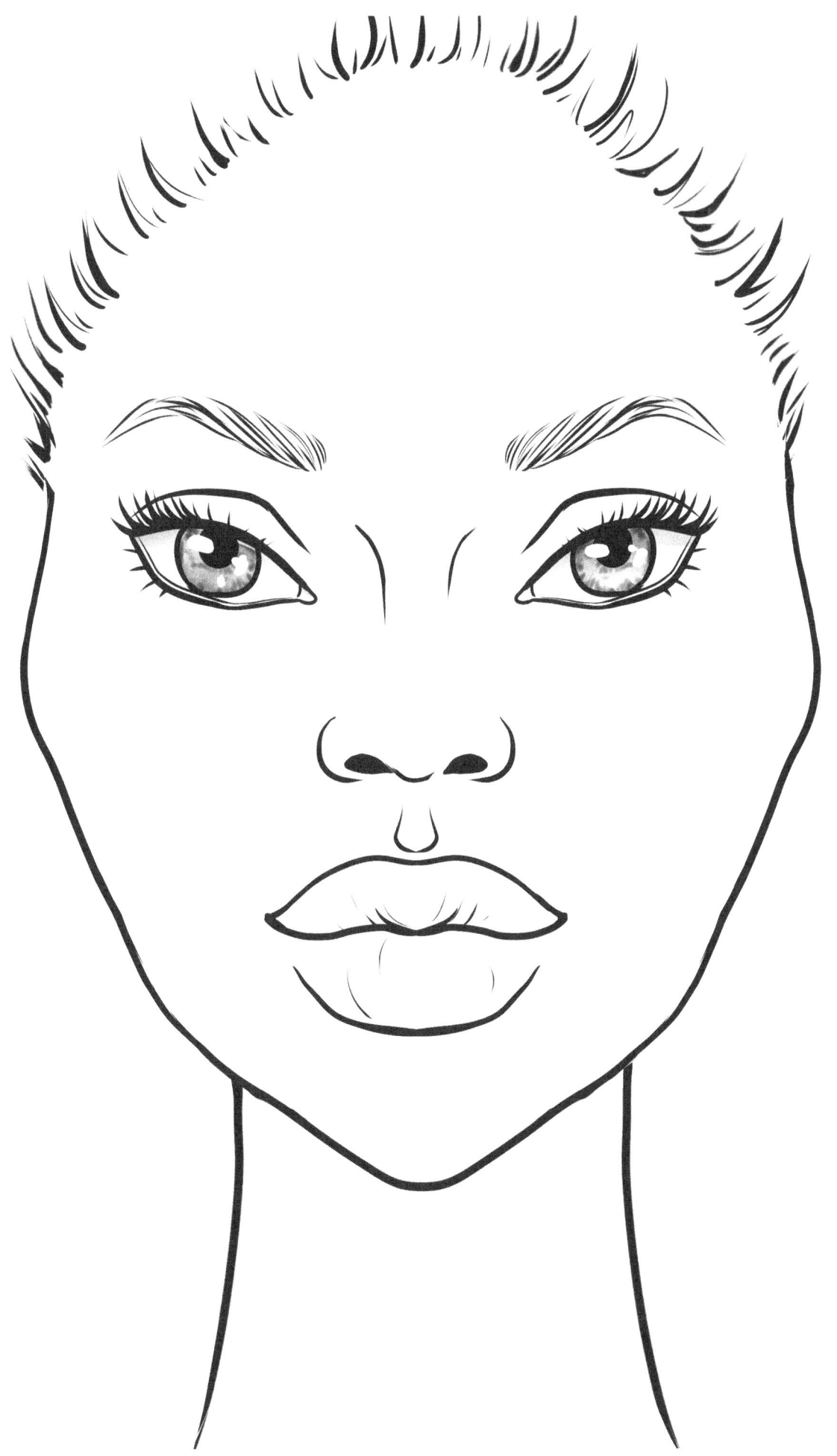

PREPARATION

Cleanser
_____

Moisturizer
_____

Primer
_____

FACE

Concealer
_____

Foundation
_____

Powder
_____

Highlighter
_____

Contour
_____

Bronzer
_____

Blush
_____

EYES

Eyeshadow lid
_____

Eyeshadow crease
_____

Eyeliner
_____

Mascara
_____

Lashes
_____

Brows
_____

LIPS

Lip color
_____

Lip liner
_____

Lip gloss
_____

OTHER

_____

_____

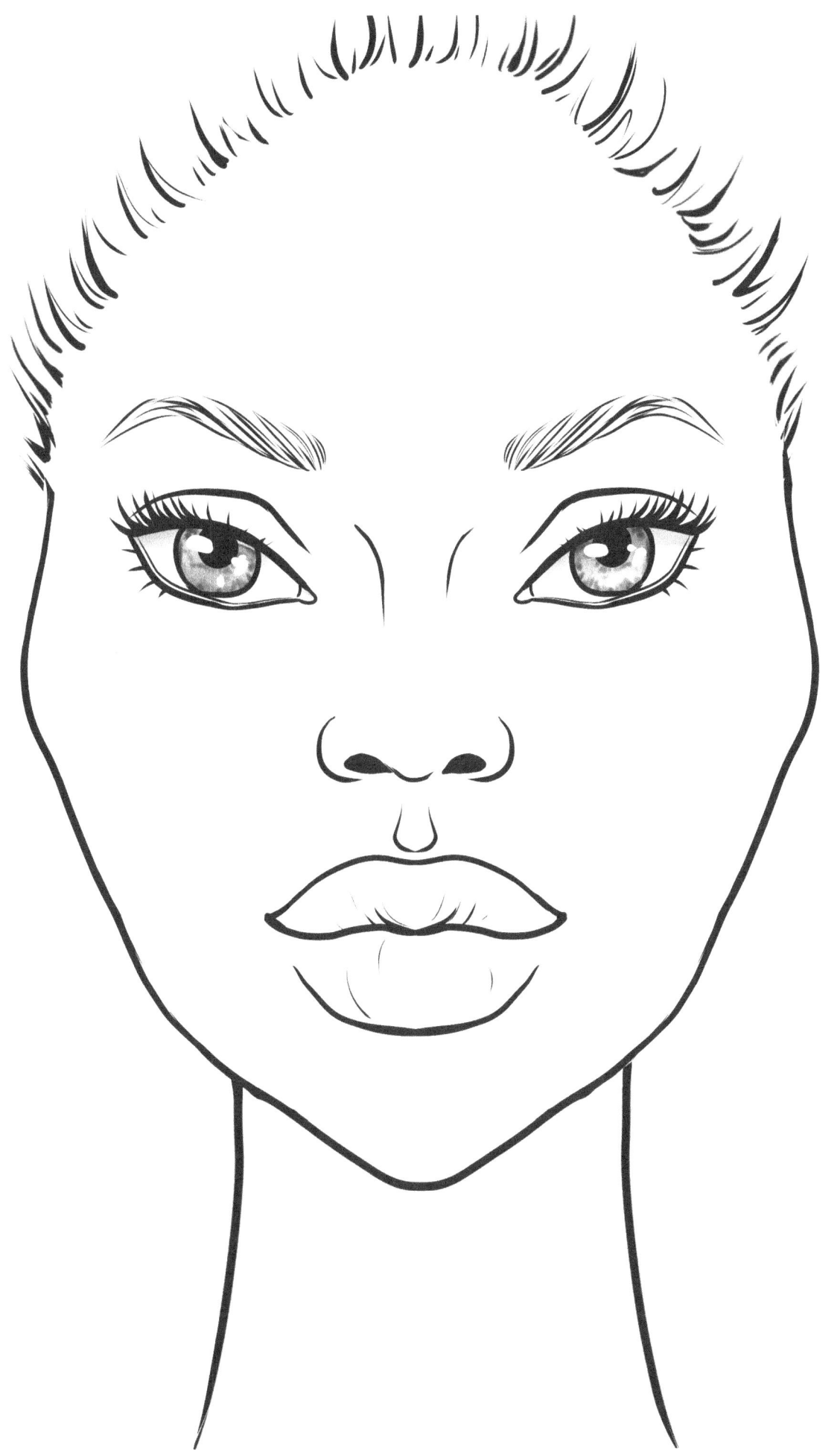

PREPARATION

Cleanser

Moisturizer

Primer

FACE

Concealer

Foundation

Powder

Highlighter

Contour

Bronzer

Blush

EYES

Eyeshadow lid

Eyeshadow crease

Eyeliner

Mascara

Lashes

Brows

LIPS

Lip color

Lip liner

Lip gloss

OTHER

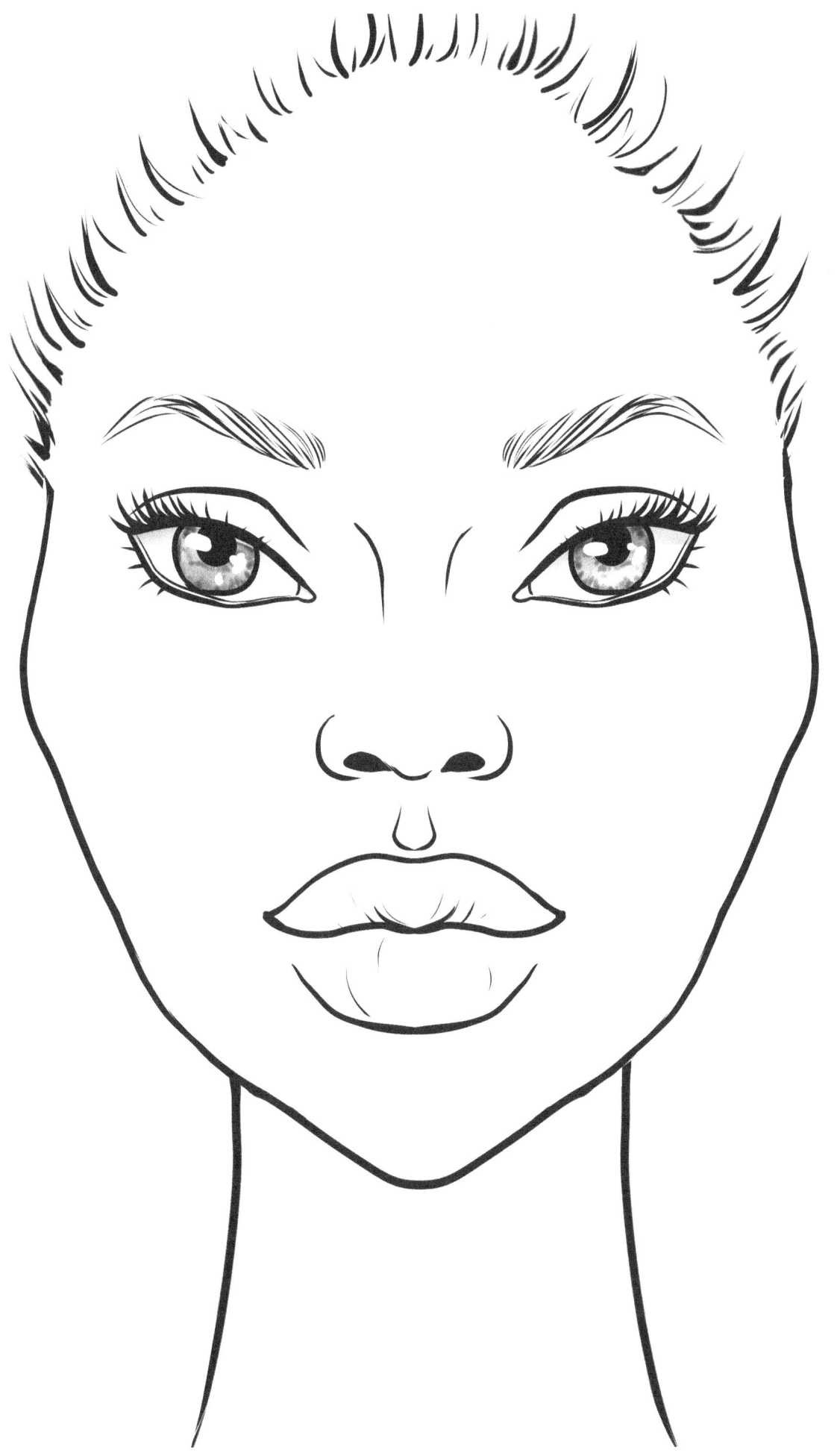

PREPARATION

Cleanser

Moisturizer

Primer

FACE

Concealer

Foundation

Powder

Highlighter

Contour

Bronzer

Blush

EYES

Eyeshadow lid

Eyeshadow crease

Eyeliner

Mascara

Lashes

Brows

LIPS

Lip color

Lip liner

Lip gloss

OTHER

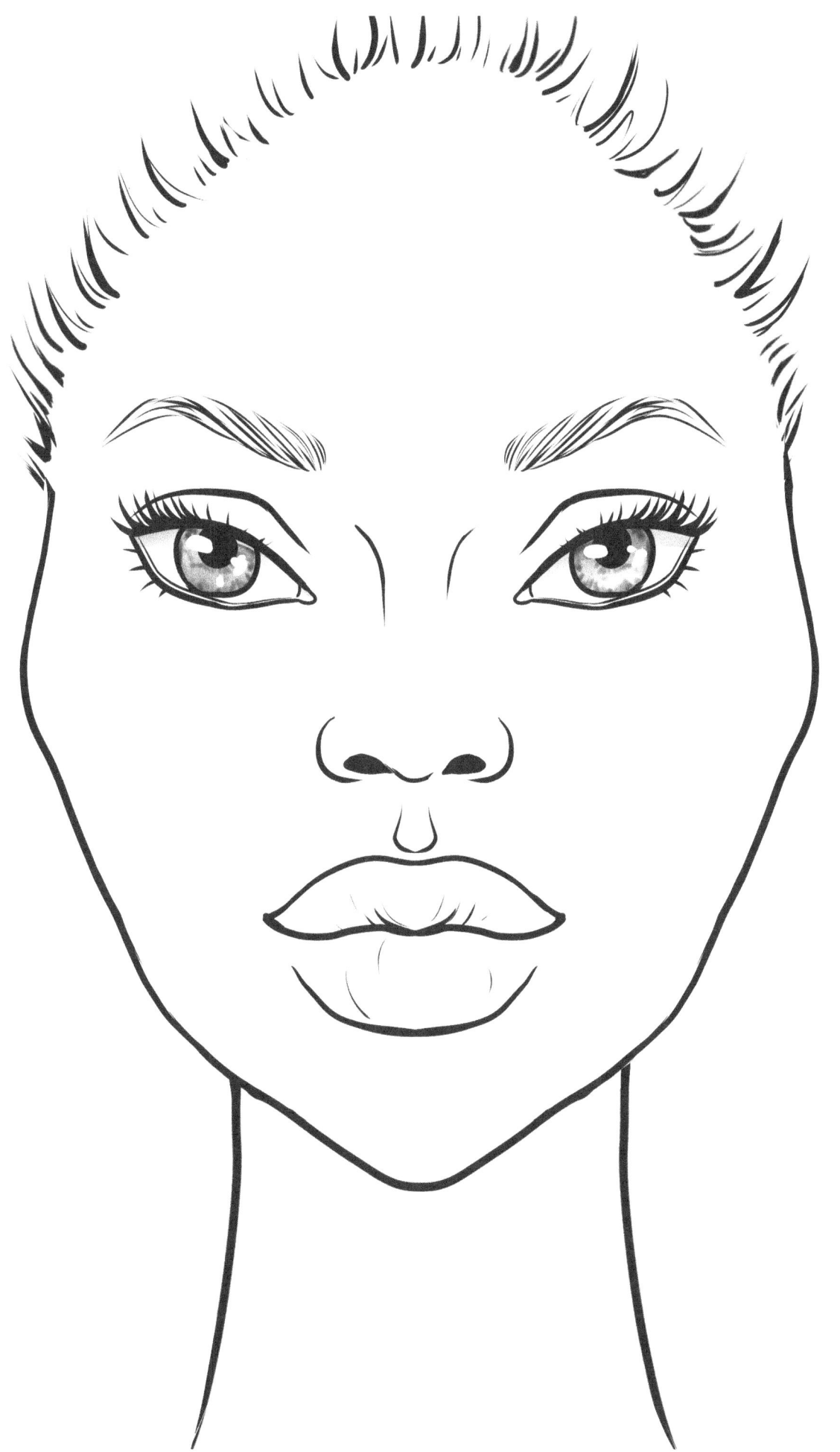

PREPARATION

Cleanser

Moisturizer

Primer

FACE

Concealer

Foundation

Powder

Highlighter

Contour

Bronzer

Blush

EYES

Eyeshadow lid

Eyeshadow crease

Eyeliner

Mascara

Lashes

Brows

LIPS

Lip color

Lip liner

Lip gloss

OTHER

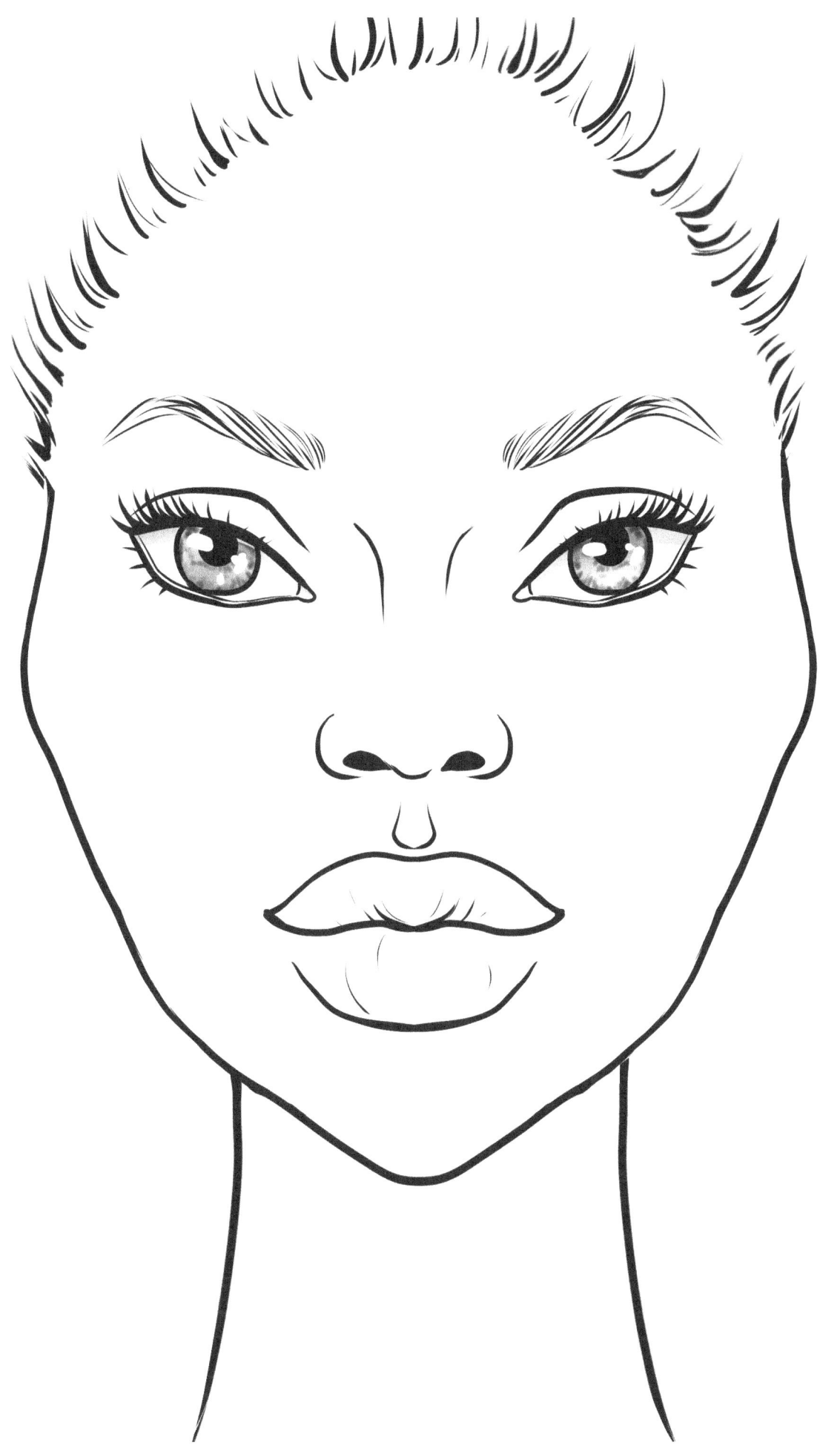

PREPARATION

Cleanser

Moisturizer

Primer

FACE

Concealer

Foundation

Powder

Highlighter

Contour

Bronzer

Blush

EYES

Eyeshadow lid

Eyeshadow crease

Eyeliner

Mascara

Lashes

Brows

LIPS

Lip color

Lip liner

Lip gloss

OTHER

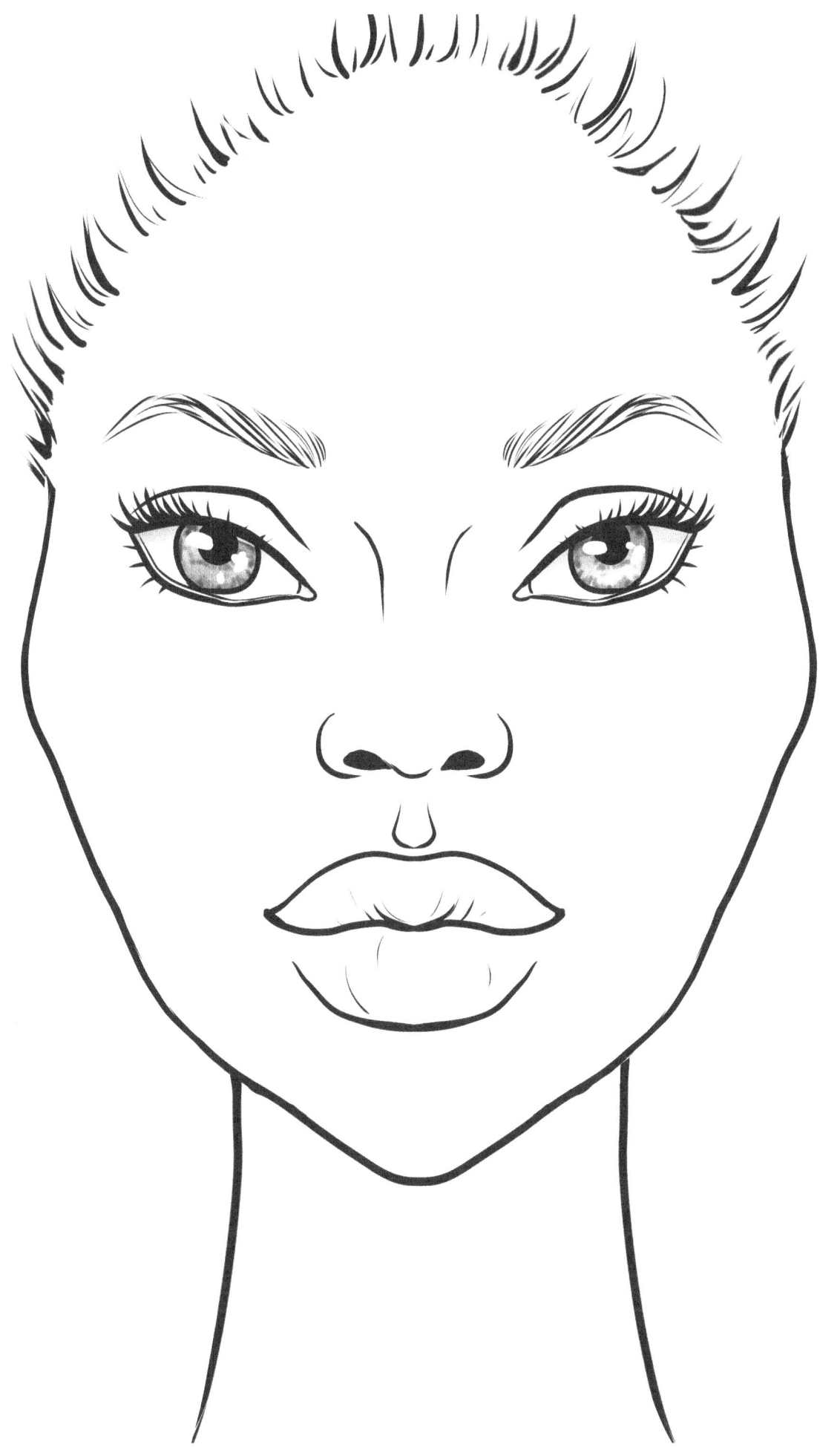

PREPARATION

Cleanser

Moisturizer

Primer

FACE

Concealer

Foundation

Powder

Highlighter

Contour

Bronzer

Blush

EYES

Eyeshadow lid

Eyeshadow crease

Eyeliner

Mascara

Lashes

Brows

LIPS

Lip color

Lip liner

Lip gloss

OTHER

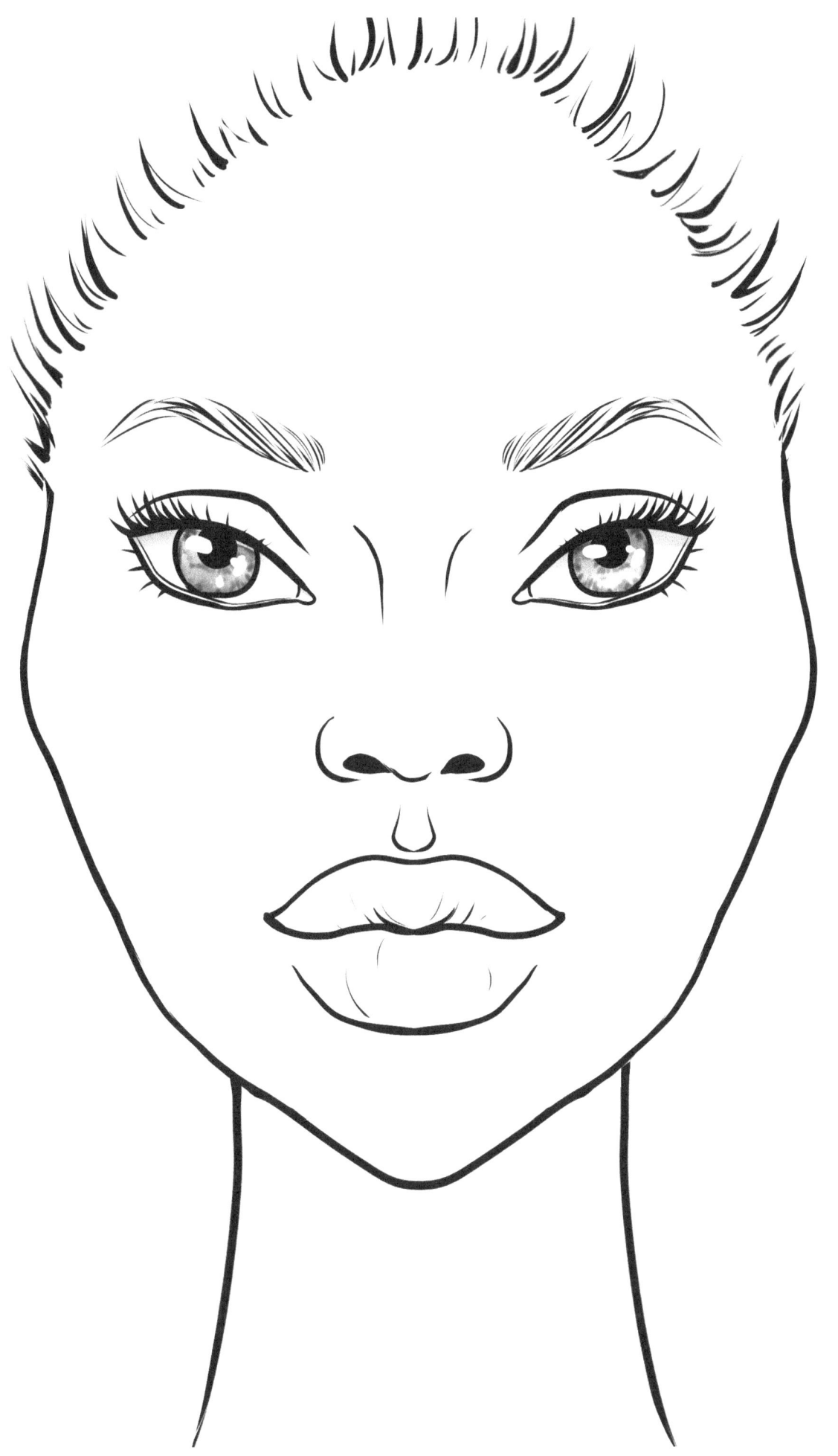

PREPARATION

Cleanser

Moisturizer

Primer

FACE

Concealer

Foundation

Powder

Highlighter

Contour

Bronzer

Blush

EYES

Eyeshadow lid

Eyeshadow crease

Eyeliner

Mascara

Lashes

Brows

LIPS

Lip color

Lip liner

Lip gloss

OTHER

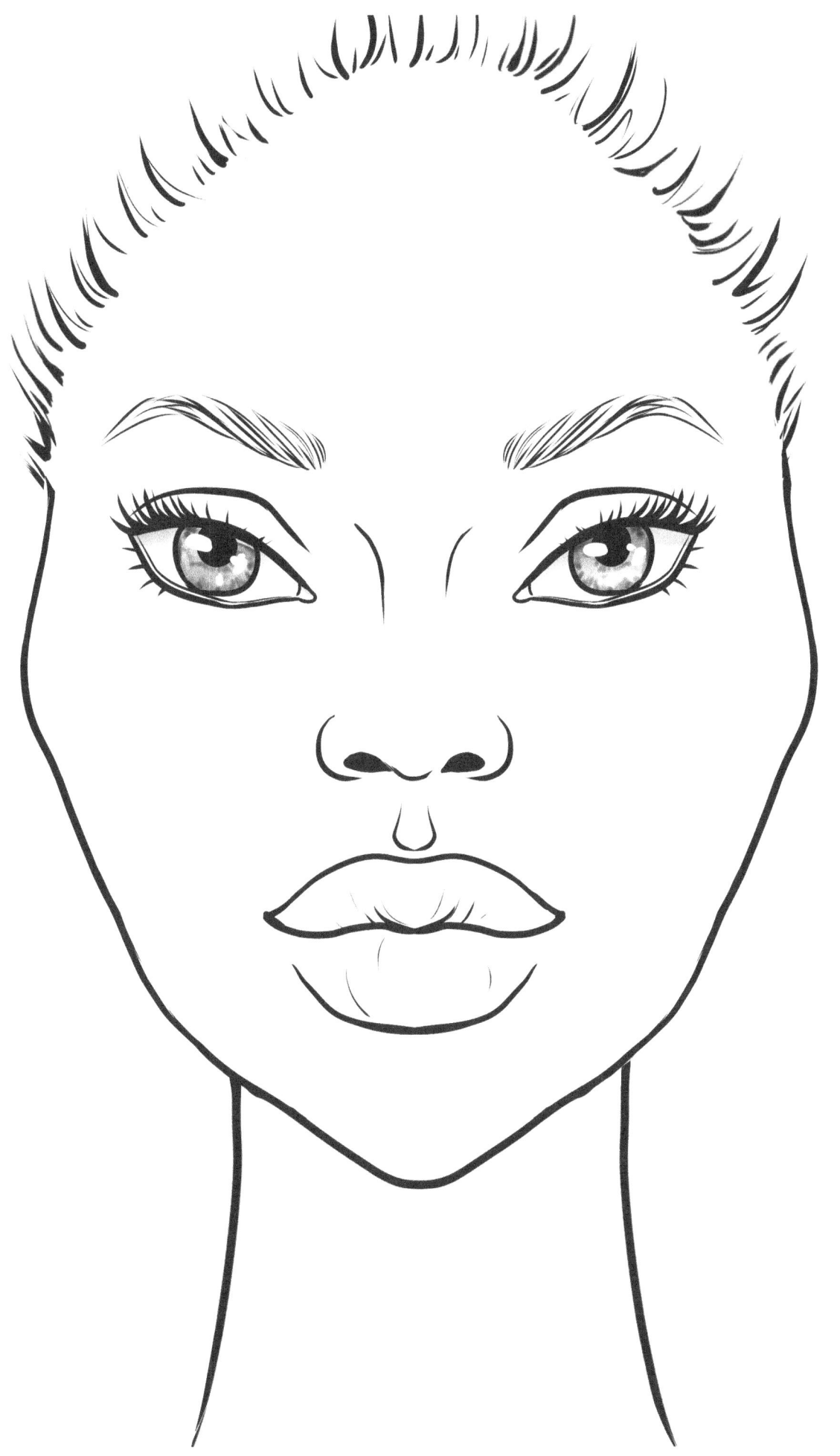

PREPARATION

Cleanser

Moisturizer

Primer

FACE

Concealer

Foundation

Powder

Highlighter

Contour

Bronzer

Blush

EYES

Eyeshadow lid

Eyeshadow crease

Eyeliner

Mascara

Lashes

Brows

LIPS

Lip color

Lip liner

Lip gloss

OTHER

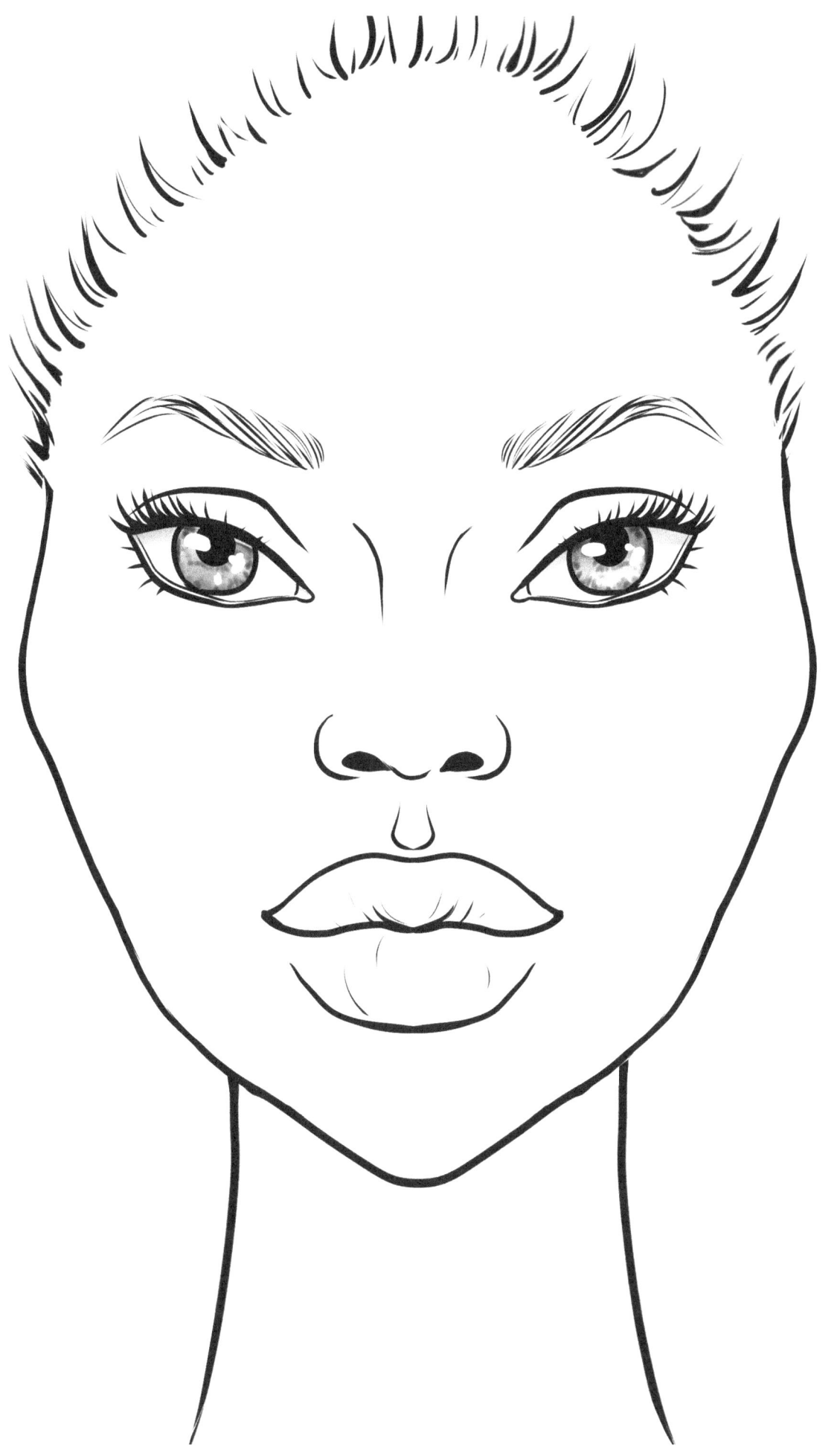

PREPARATION

Cleanser

_____

Moisturizer

_____

Primer

_____

FACE

Concealer

_____

Foundation

_____

Powder

_____

Highlighter

_____

Contour

_____

Bronzer

_____

Blush

_____

EYES

Eyeshadow lid

_____

Eyeshadow crease

_____

Eyeliner

_____

Mascara

_____

Lashes

_____

Brows

_____

LIPS

Lip color

_____

Lip liner

_____

Lip gloss

_____

OTHER

_____

_____

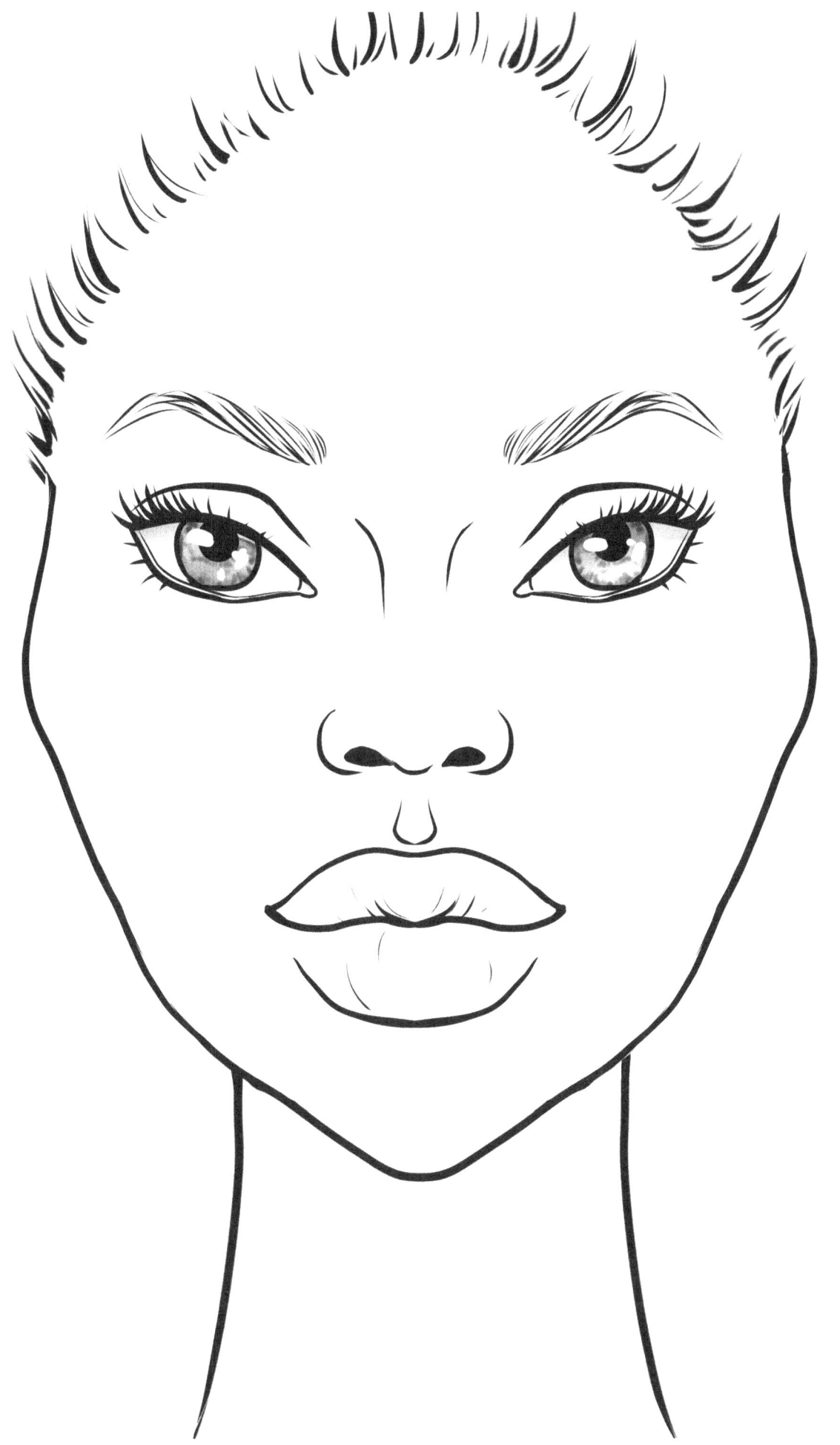

PREPARATION

Cleanser

Moisturizer

Primer

FACE

Concealer

Foundation

Powder

Highlighter

Contour

Bronzer

Blush

EYES

Eyeshadow lid

Eyeshadow crease

Eyeliner

Mascara

Lashes

Brows

LIPS

Lip color

Lip liner

Lip gloss

OTHER

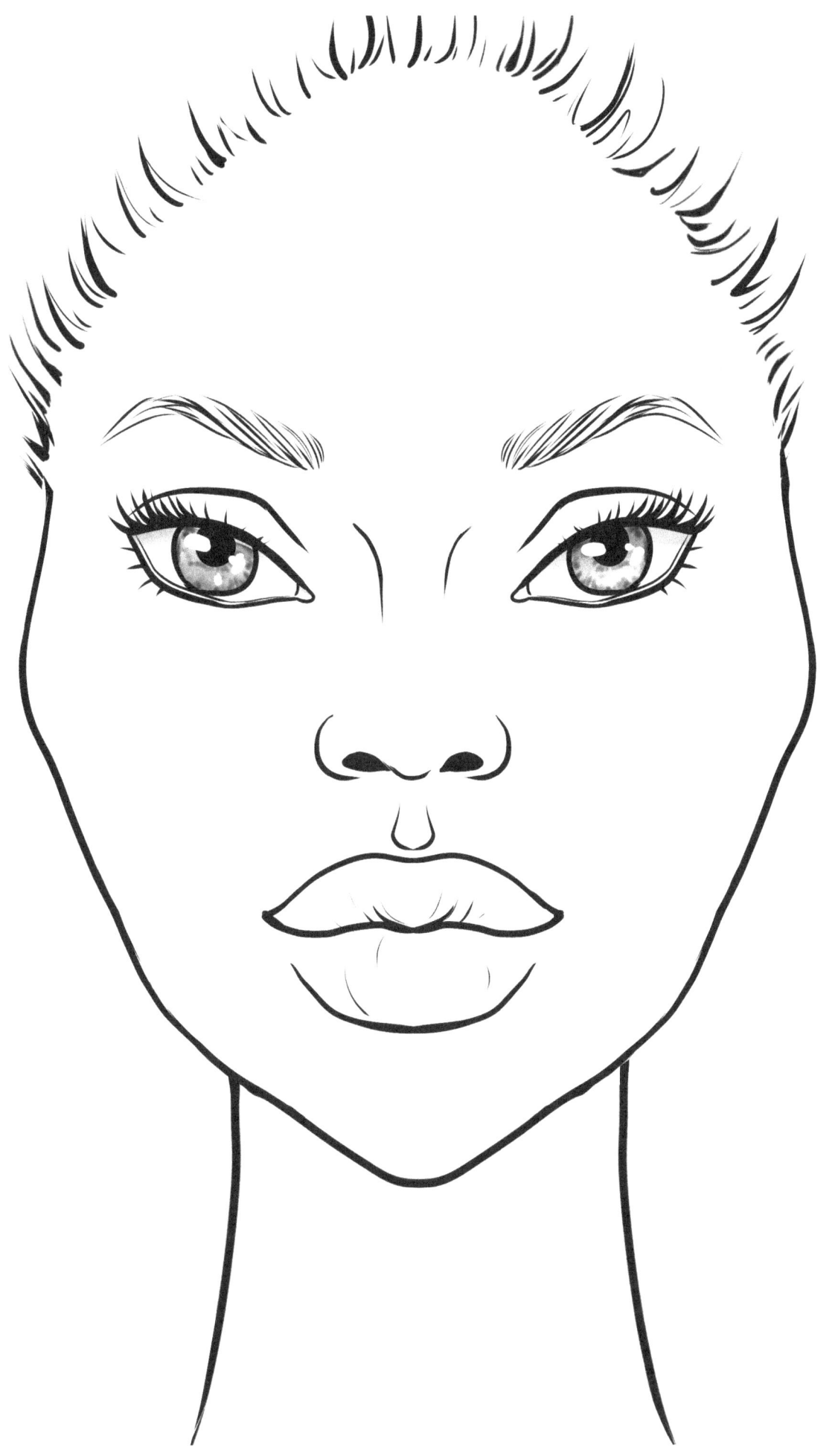

PREPARATION

Cleanser

Moisturizer

Primer

FACE

Concealer

Foundation

Powder

Highlighter

Contour

Bronzer

Blush

EYES

Eyeshadow lid

Eyeshadow crease

Eyeliner

Mascara

Lashes

Brows

LIPS

Lip color

Lip liner

Lip gloss

OTHER

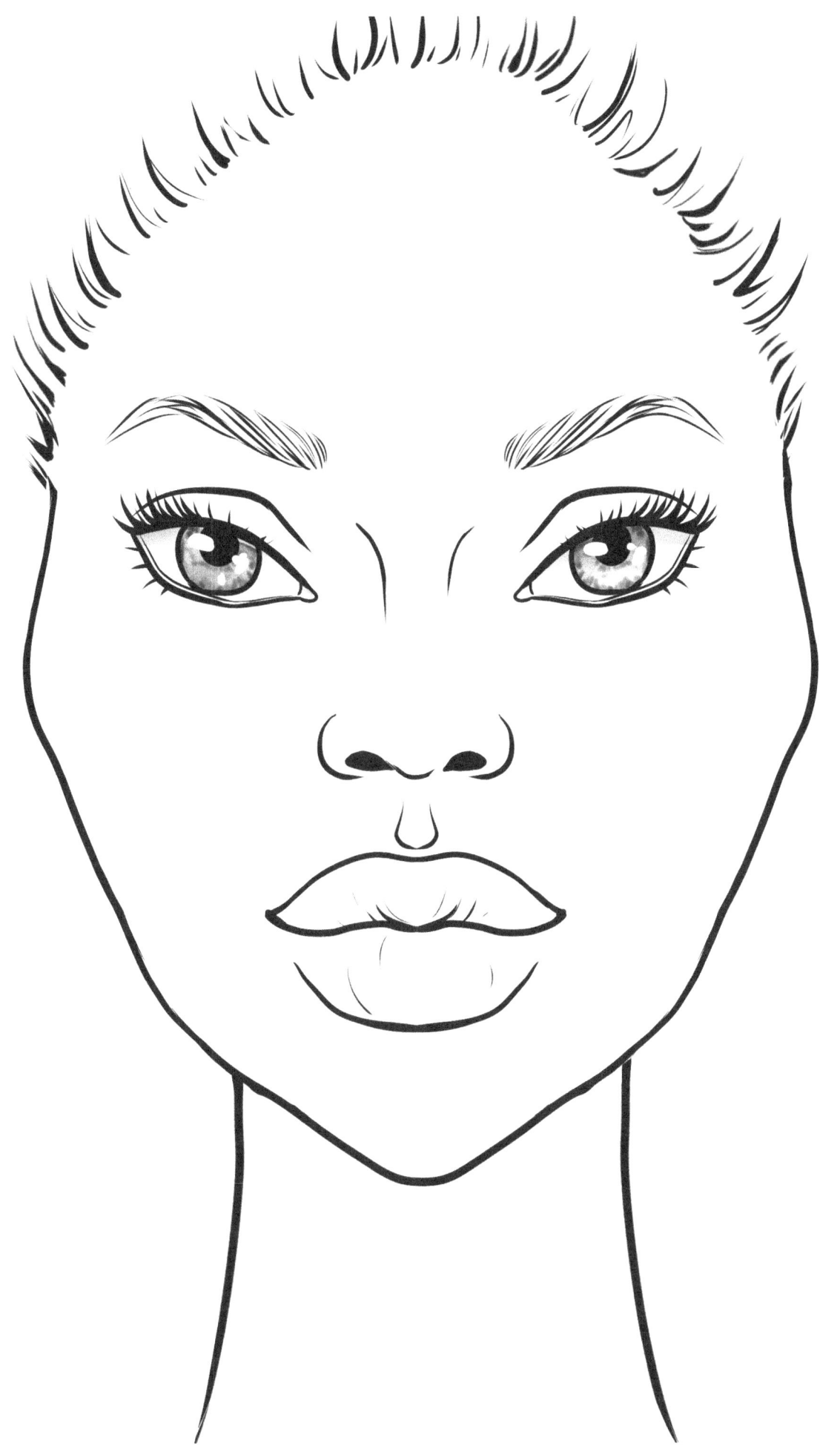

PREPARATION

Cleanser

Moisturizer

Primer

FACE

Concealer

Foundation

Powder

Highlighter

Contour

Bronzer

Blush

EYES

Eyeshadow lid

Eyeshadow crease

Eyeliner

Mascara

Lashes

Brows

LIPS

Lip color

Lip liner

Lip gloss

OTHER

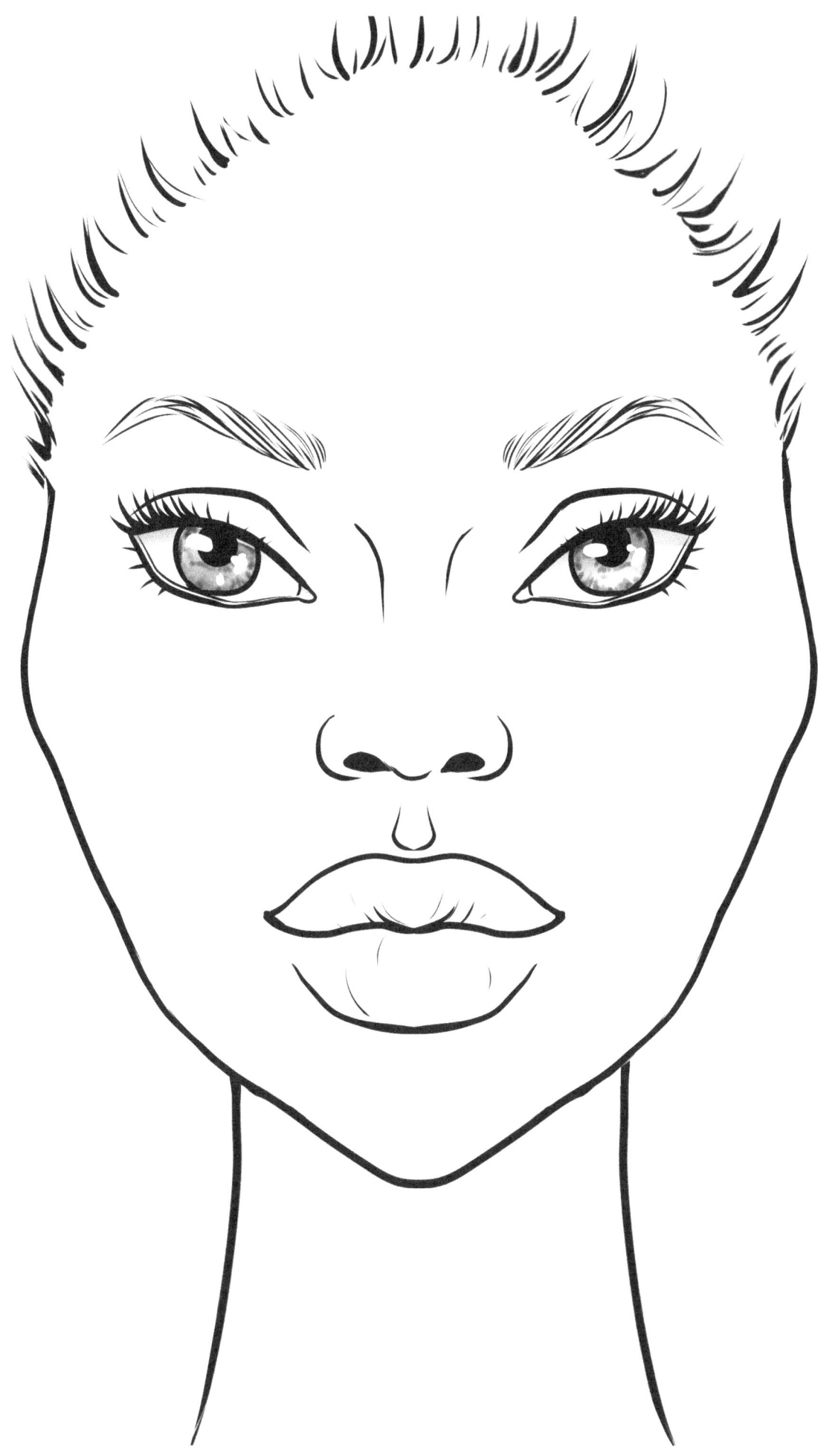

PREPARATION

Cleanser

Moisturizer

Primer

FACE

Concealer

Foundation

Powder

Highlighter

Contour

Bronzer

Blush

EYES

Eyeshadow lid

Eyeshadow crease

Eyeliner

Mascara

Lashes

Brows

LIPS

Lip color

Lip liner

Lip gloss

OTHER

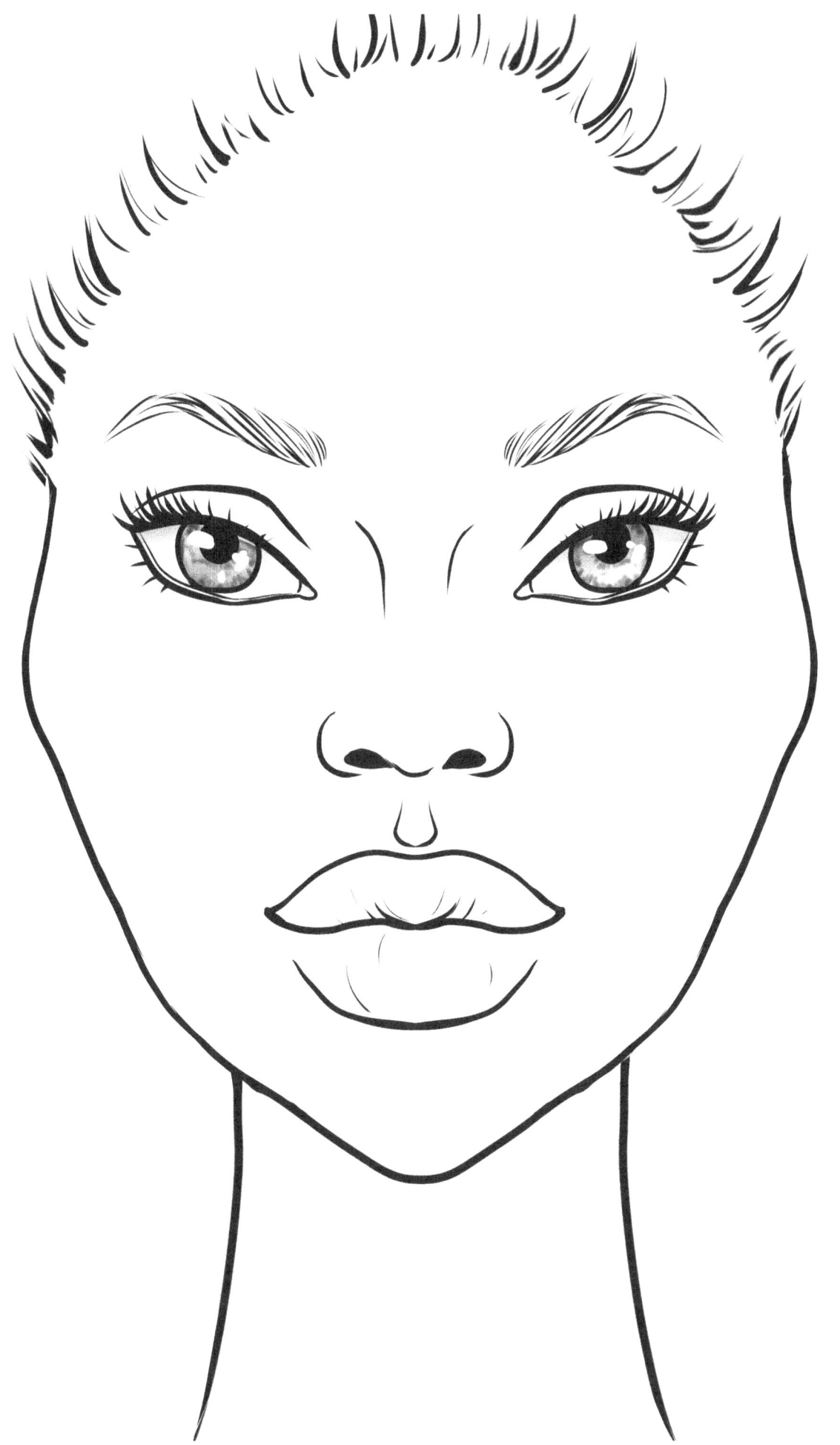

PREPARATION

Cleanser

Moisturizer

Primer

FACE

Concealer

Foundation

Powder

Highlighter

Contour

Bronzer

Blush

EYES

Eyeshadow lid

Eyeshadow crease

Eyeliner

Mascara

Lashes

Brows

LIPS

Lip color

Lip liner

Lip gloss

OTHER

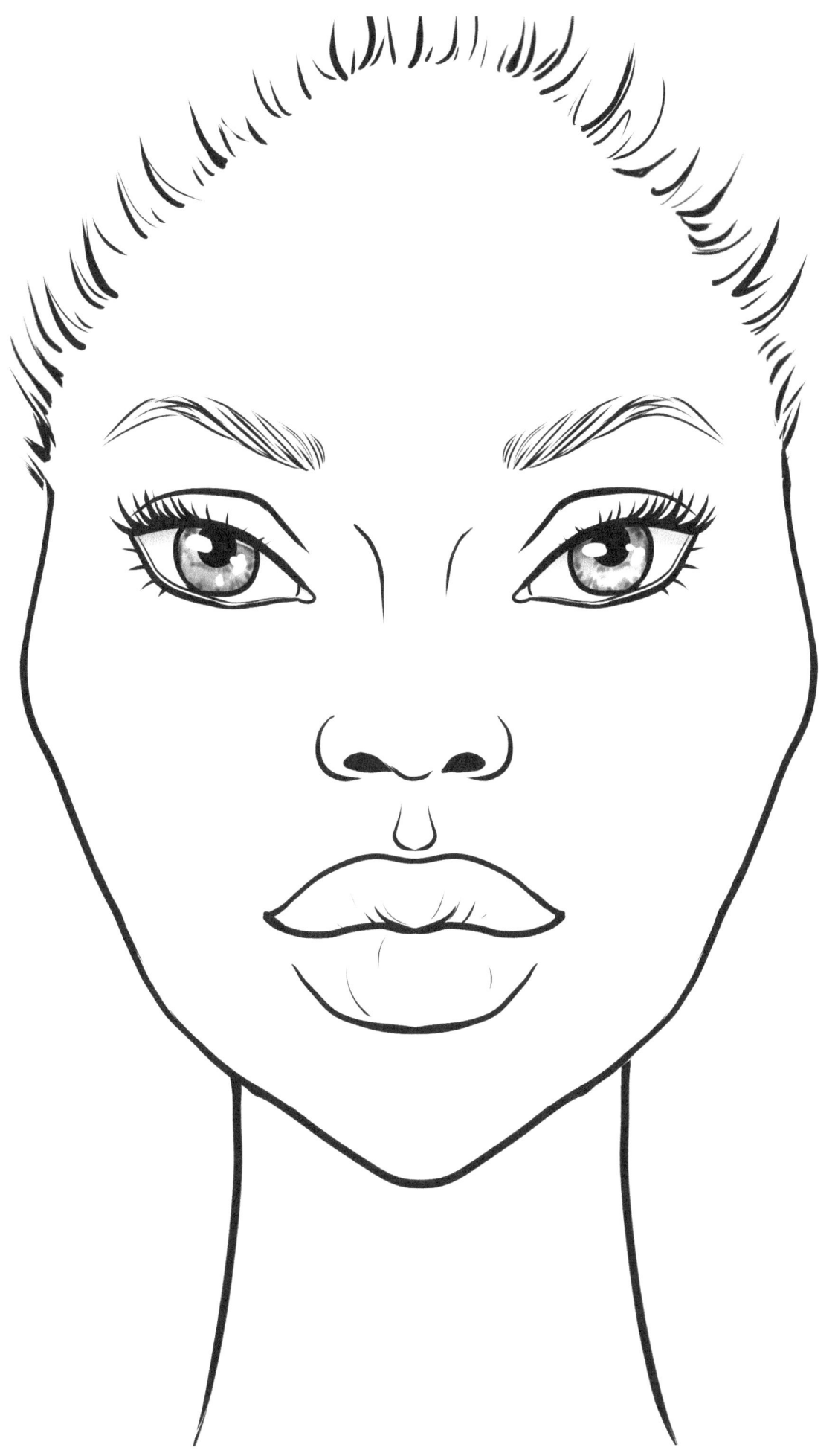

PREPARATION

Cleanser

Moisturizer

Primer

FACE

Concealer

Foundation

Powder

Highlighter

Contour

Bronzer

Blush

EYES

Eyeshadow lid

Eyeshadow crease

Eyeliner

Mascara

Lashes

Brows

LIPS

Lip color

Lip liner

Lip gloss

OTHER

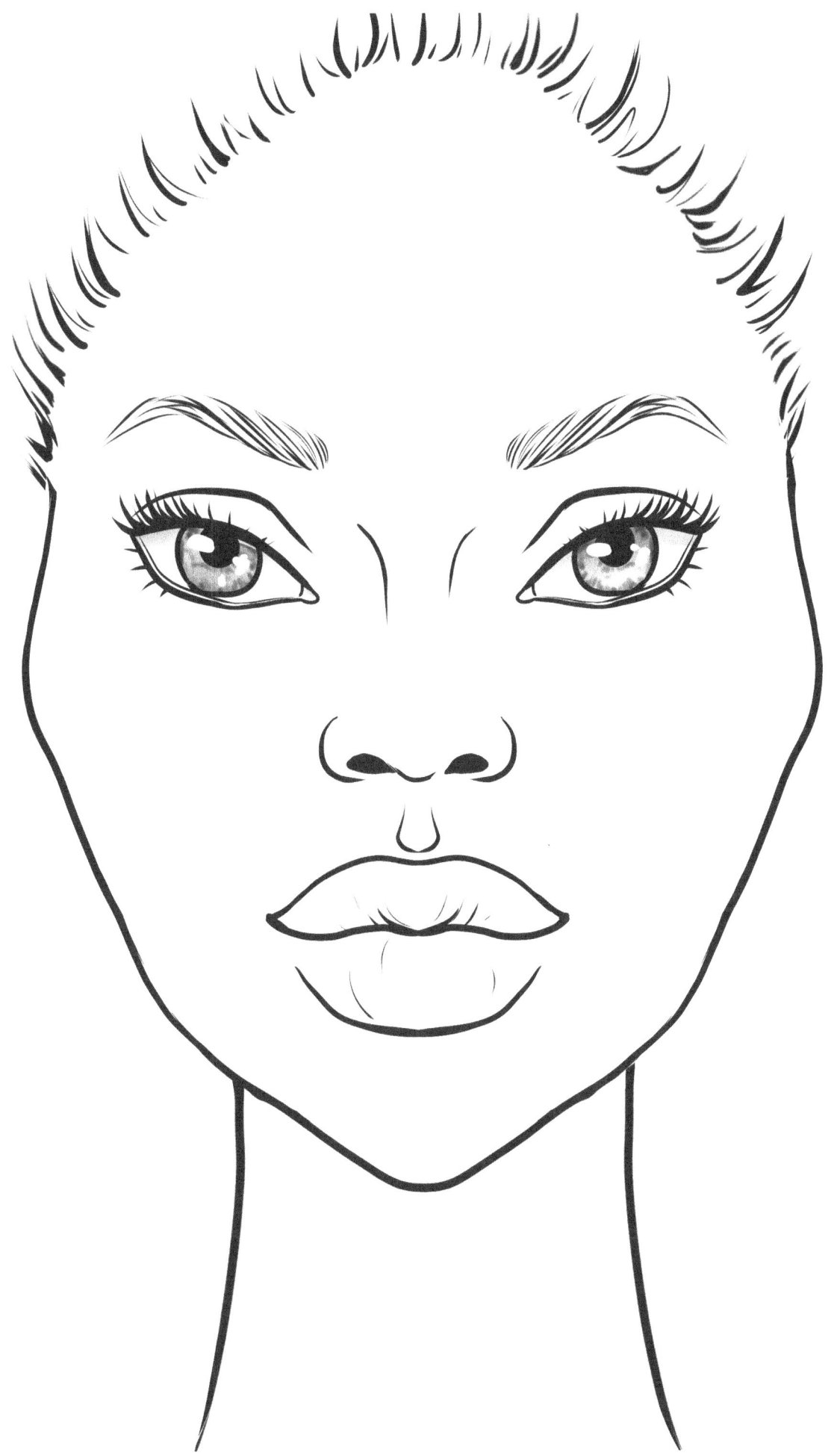

PREPARATION

Cleanser

Moisturizer

Primer

FACE

Concealer

Foundation

Powder

Highlighter

Contour

Bronzer

Blush

EYES

Eyeshadow lid

Eyeshadow crease

Eyeliner

Mascara

Lashes

Brows

LIPS

Lip color

Lip liner

Lip gloss

OTHER

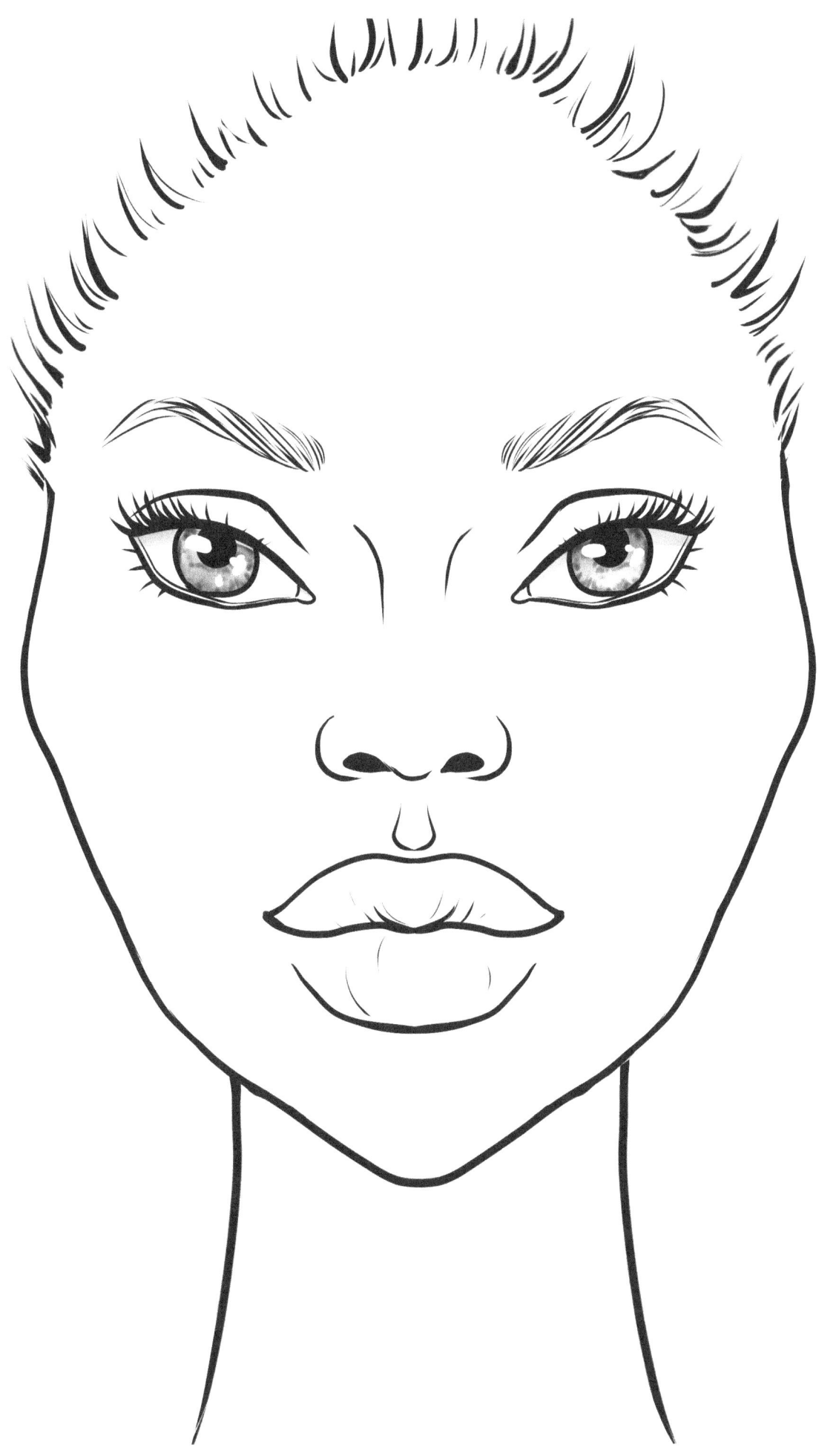

ONE EYE OPENED, ONE EYE CLOSED FACE CHARTS

PREPARATION

Cleanser

Moisturizer

Primer

FACE

Concealer

Foundation

Powder

Highlighter

Contour

Bronzer

Blush

EYES

Eyeshadow lid

Eyeshadow crease

Eyeliner

Mascara

Lashes

Brows

LIPS

Lip color

Lip liner

Lip gloss

OTHER

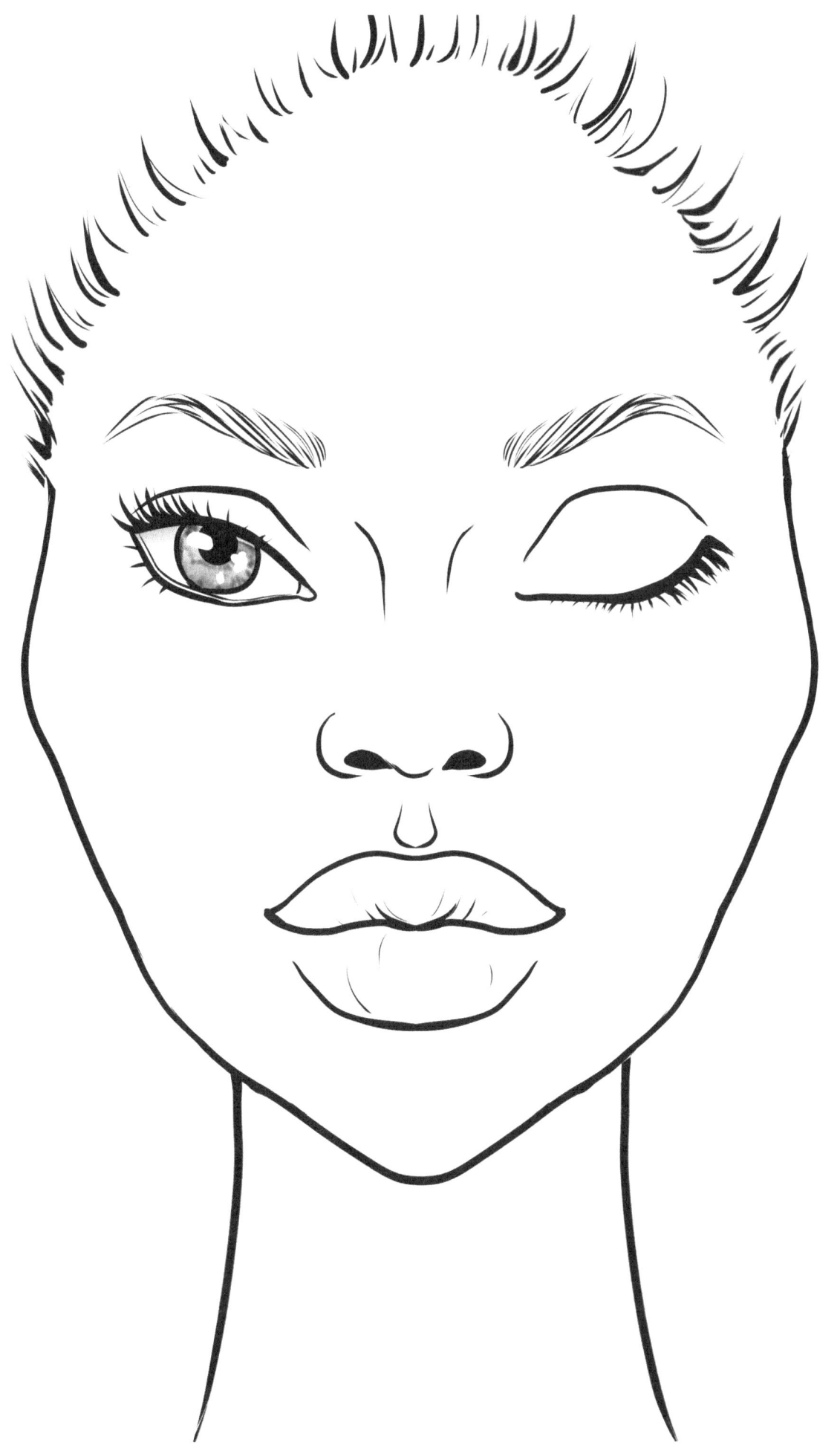

PREPARATION

Cleanser

Moisturizer

Primer

FACE

Concealer

Foundation

Powder

Highlighter

Contour

Bronzer

Blush

EYES

Eyeshadow lid

Eyeshadow crease

Eyeliner

Mascara

Lashes

Brows

LIPS

Lip color

Lip liner

Lip gloss

OTHER

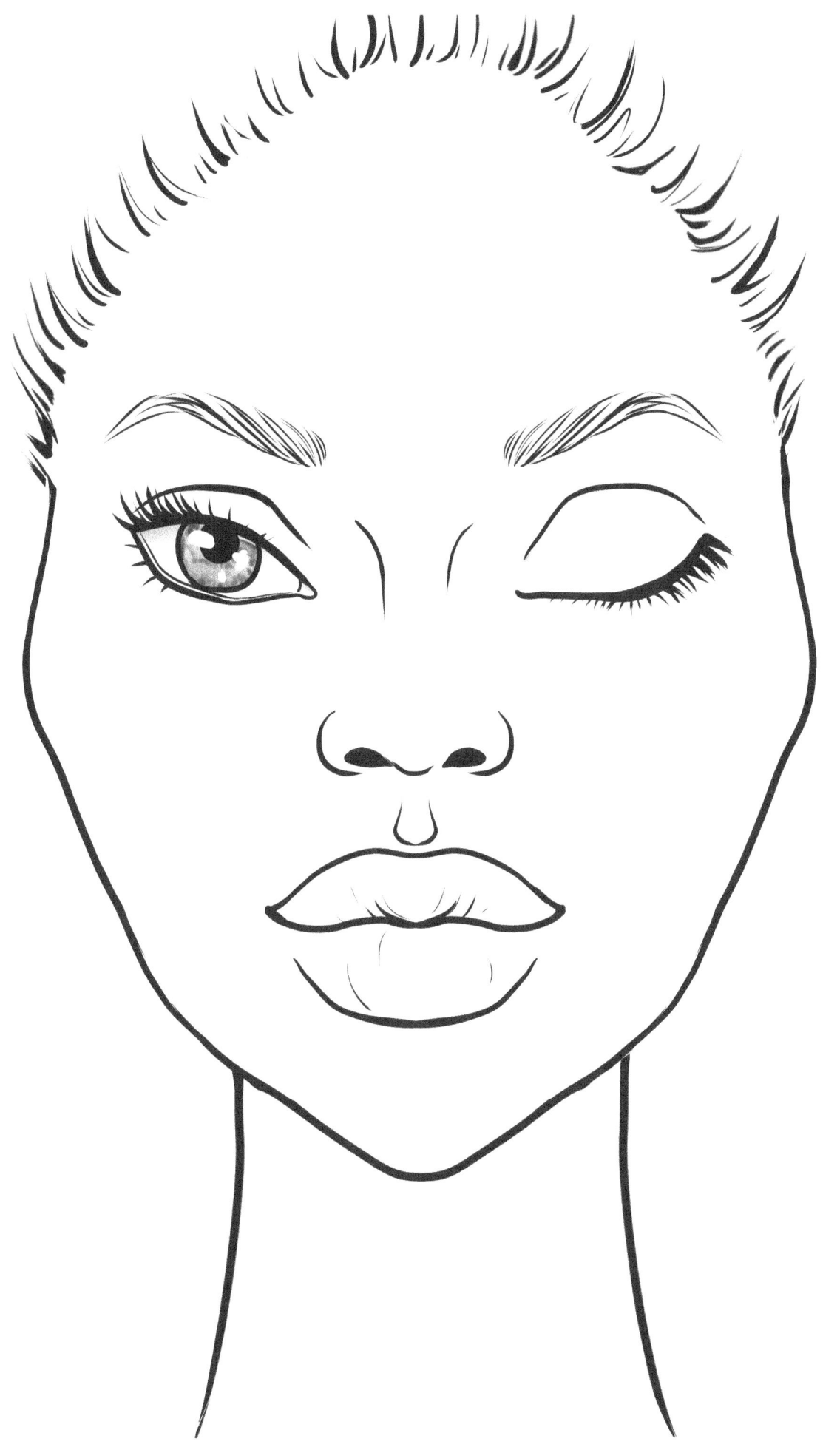

PREPARATION

Cleanser

Moisturizer

Primer

FACE

Concealer

Foundation

Powder

Highlighter

Contour

Bronzer

Blush

EYES

Eyeshadow lid

Eyeshadow crease

Eyeliner

Mascara

Lashes

Brows

LIPS

Lip color

Lip liner

Lip gloss

OTHER

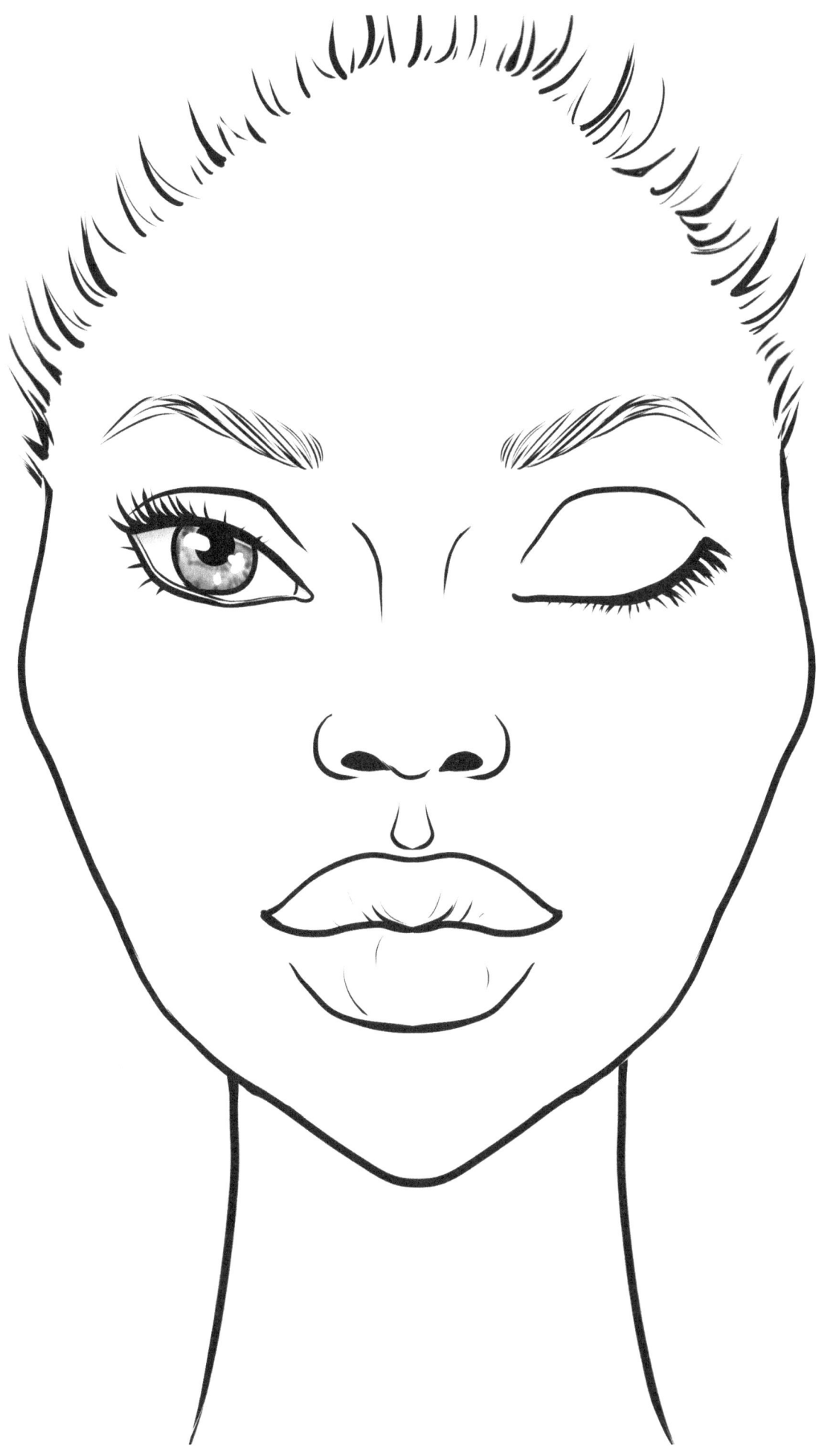

PREPARATION

Cleanser

Moisturizer

Primer

FACE

Concealer

Foundation

Powder

Highlighter

Contour

Bronzer

Blush

EYES

Eyeshadow lid

Eyeshadow crease

Eyeliner

Mascara

Lashes

Brows

LIPS

Lip color

Lip liner

Lip gloss

OTHER

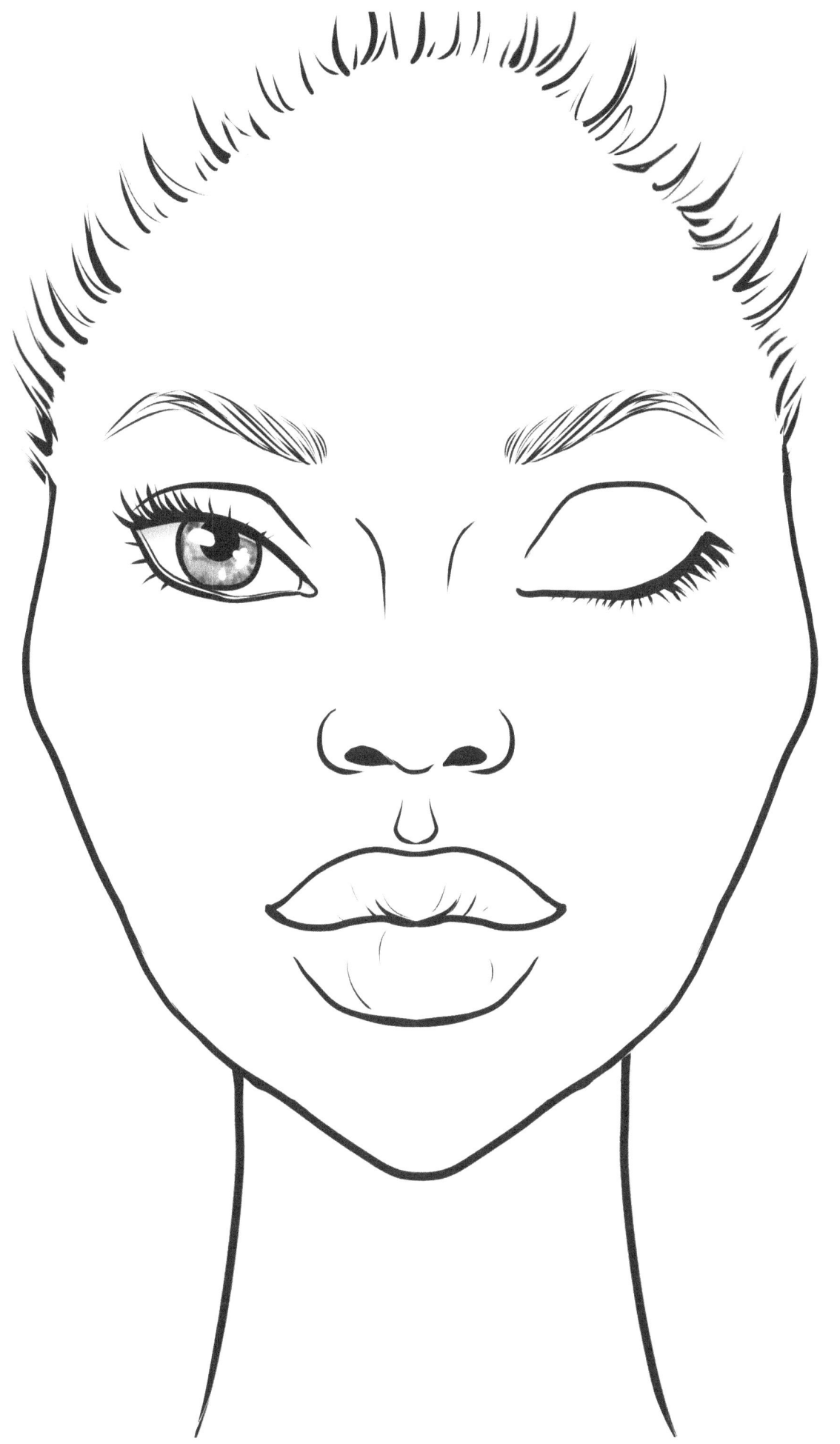

PREPARATION

Cleanser

Moisturizer

Primer

FACE

Concealer

Foundation

Powder

Highlighter

Contour

Bronzer

Blush

EYES

Eyeshadow lid

Eyeshadow crease

Eyeliner

Mascara

Lashes

Brows

LIPS

Lip color

Lip liner

Lip gloss

OTHER

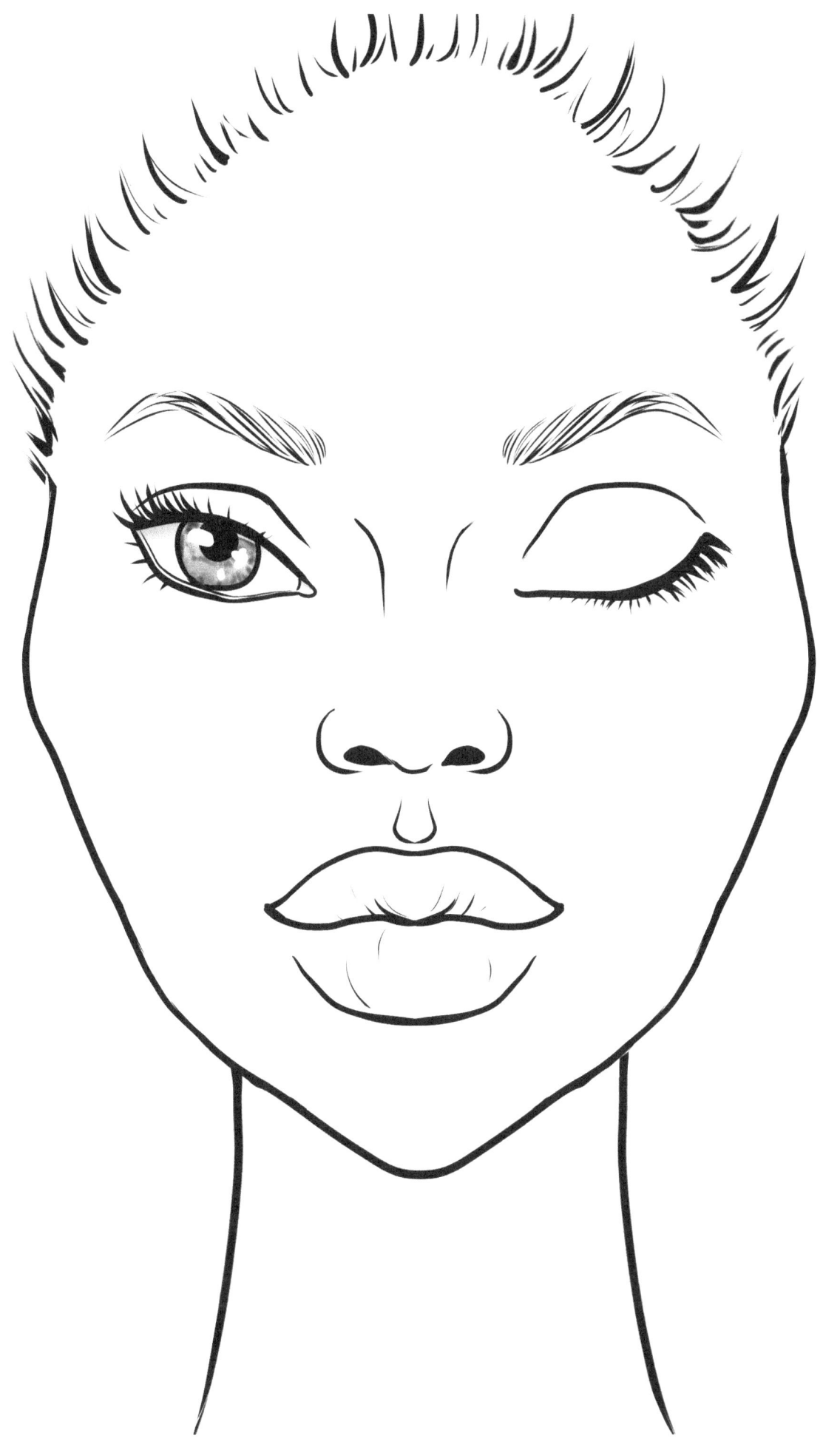

PREPARATION

Cleanser
_____

Moisturizer
_____

Primer
_____

FACE

Concealer
_____

Foundation
_____

Powder
_____

Highlighter
_____

Contour
_____

Bronzer
_____

Blush
_____

EYES

Eyeshadow lid
_____

Eyeshadow crease
_____

Eyeliner
_____

Mascara
_____

Lashes
_____

Brows
_____

LIPS

Lip color
_____

Lip liner
_____

Lip gloss
_____

OTHER

_____

_____

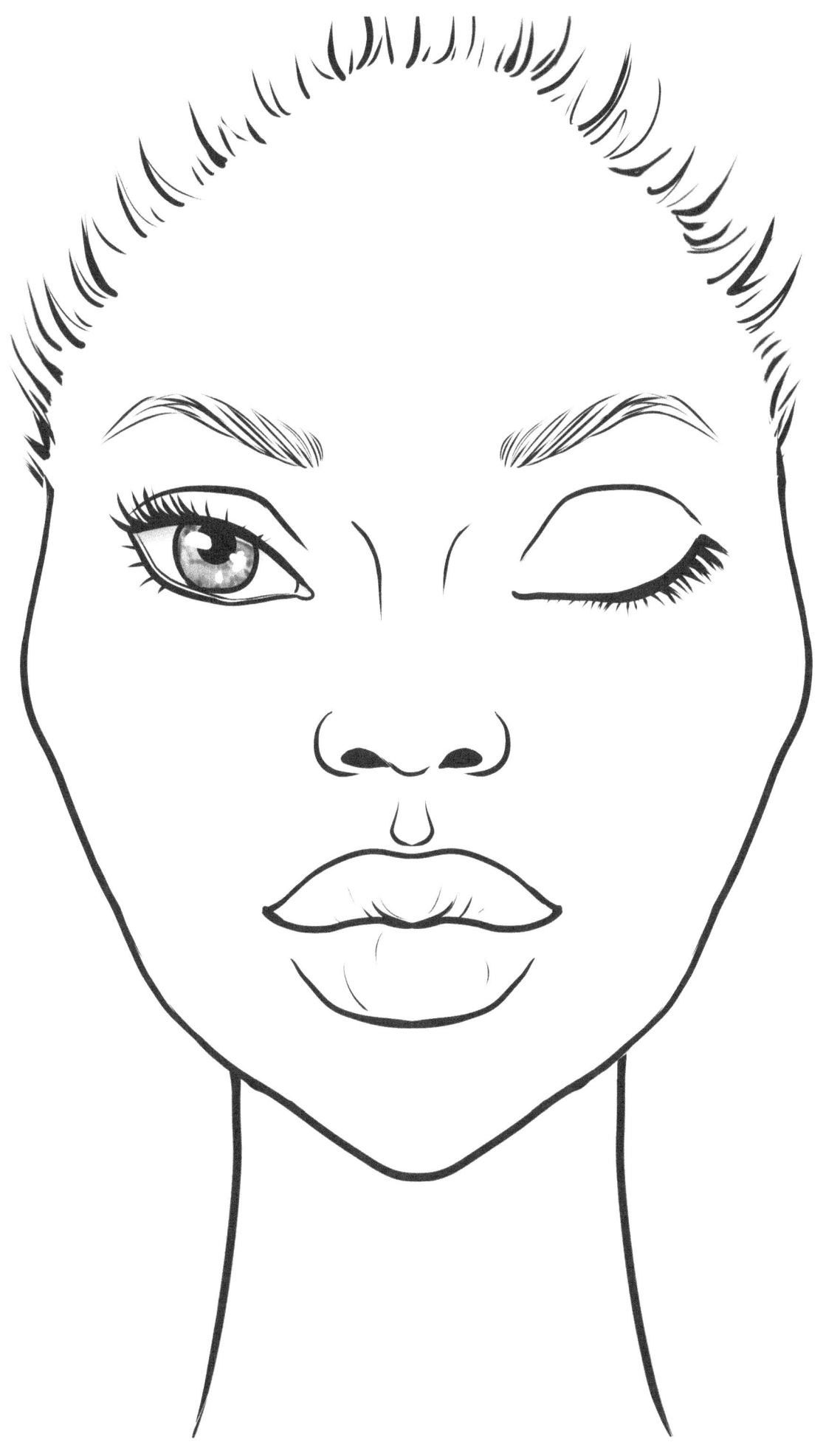

PREPARATION

Cleanser

Moisturizer

Primer

FACE

Concealer

Foundation

Powder

Highlighter

Contour

Bronzer

Blush

EYES

Eyeshadow lid

Eyeshadow crease

Eyeliner

Mascara

Lashes

Brows

LIPS

Lip color

Lip liner

Lip gloss

OTHER

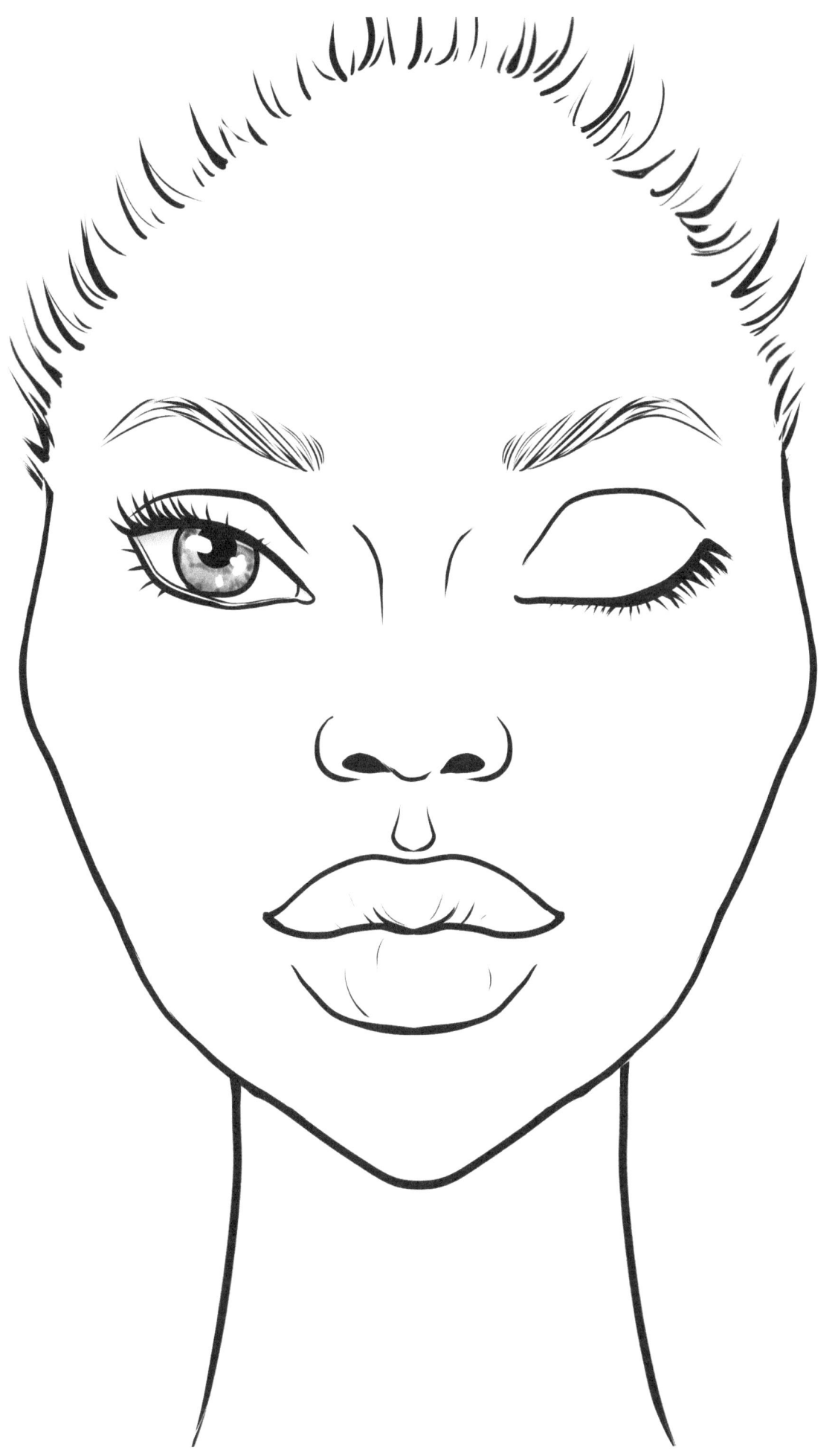

PREPARATION

Cleanser

Moisturizer

Primer

FACE

Concealer

Foundation

Powder

Highlighter

Contour

Bronzer

Blush

EYES

Eyeshadow lid

Eyeshadow crease

Eyeliner

Mascara

Lashes

Brows

LIPS

Lip color

Lip liner

Lip gloss

OTHER

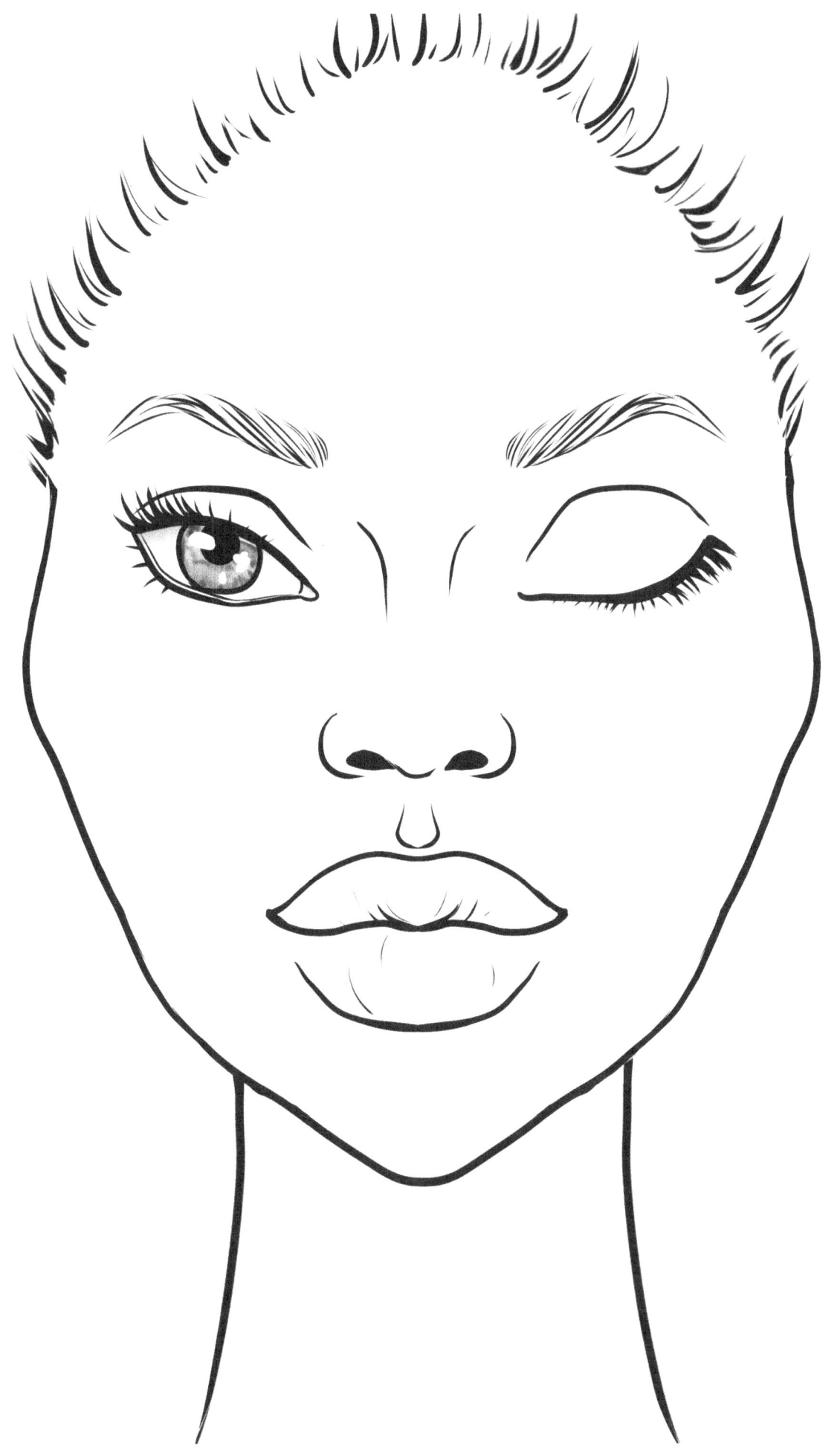

PREPARATION

Cleanser

Moisturizer

Primer

FACE

Concealer

Foundation

Powder

Highlighter

Contour

Bronzer

Blush

EYES

Eyeshadow lid

Eyeshadow crease

Eyeliner

Mascara

Lashes

Brows

LIPS

Lip color

Lip liner

Lip gloss

OTHER

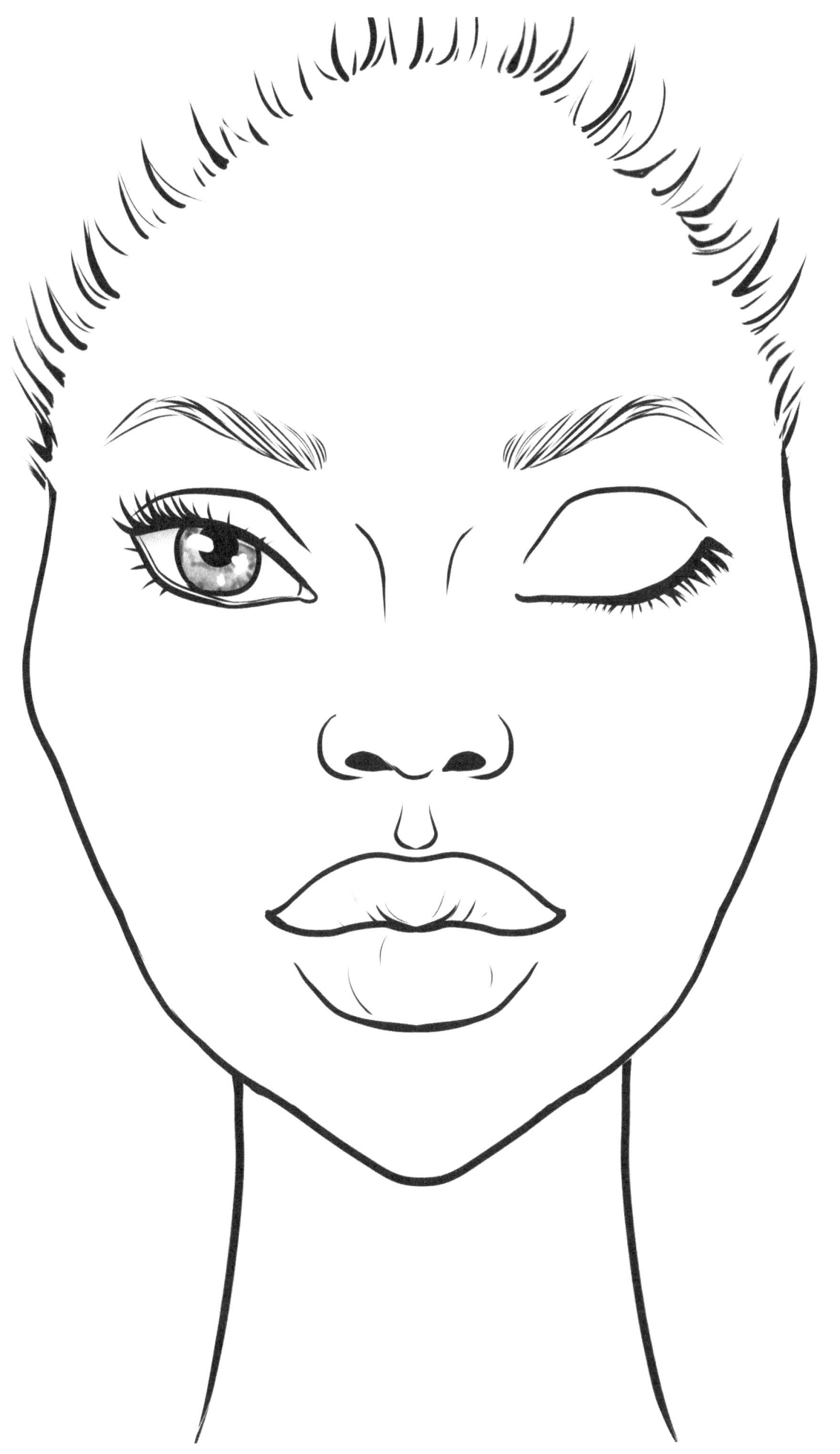

PREPARATION

Cleanser

_____

Moisturizer

_____

Primer

_____

FACE

Concealer

_____

Foundation

_____

Powder

_____

Highlighter

_____

Contour

_____

Bronzer

_____

Blush

_____

EYES

Eyeshadow lid

_____

Eyeshadow crease

_____

Eyeliner

_____

Mascara

_____

Lashes

_____

Brows

_____

LIPS

Lip color

_____

Lip liner

_____

Lip gloss

_____

OTHER

_____

_____

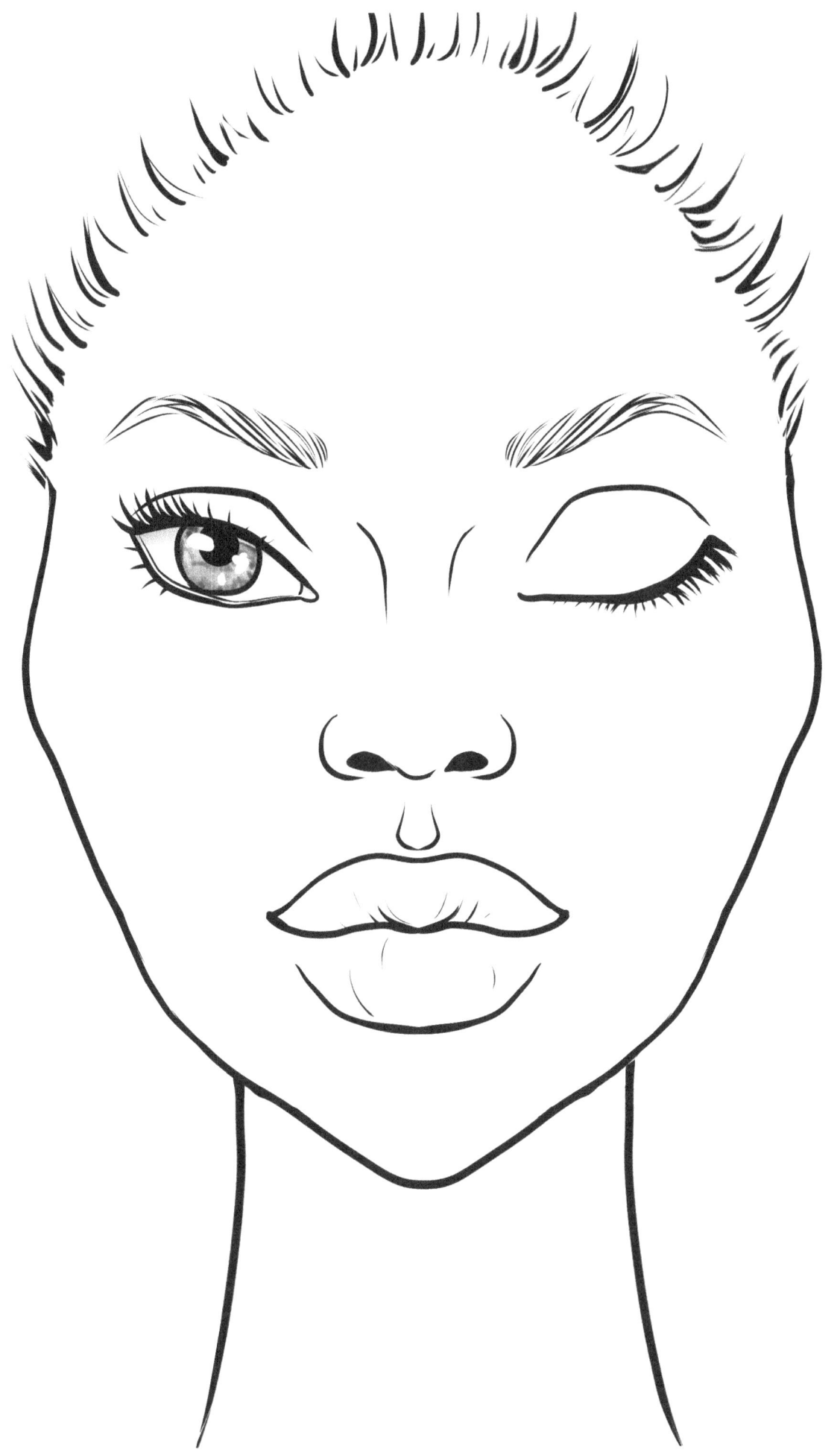

PREPARATION

Cleanser

Moisturizer

Primer

FACE

Concealer

Foundation

Powder

Highlighter

Contour

Bronzer

Blush

EYES

Eyeshadow lid

Eyeshadow crease

Eyeliner

Mascara

Lashes

Brows

LIPS

Lip color

Lip liner

Lip gloss

OTHER

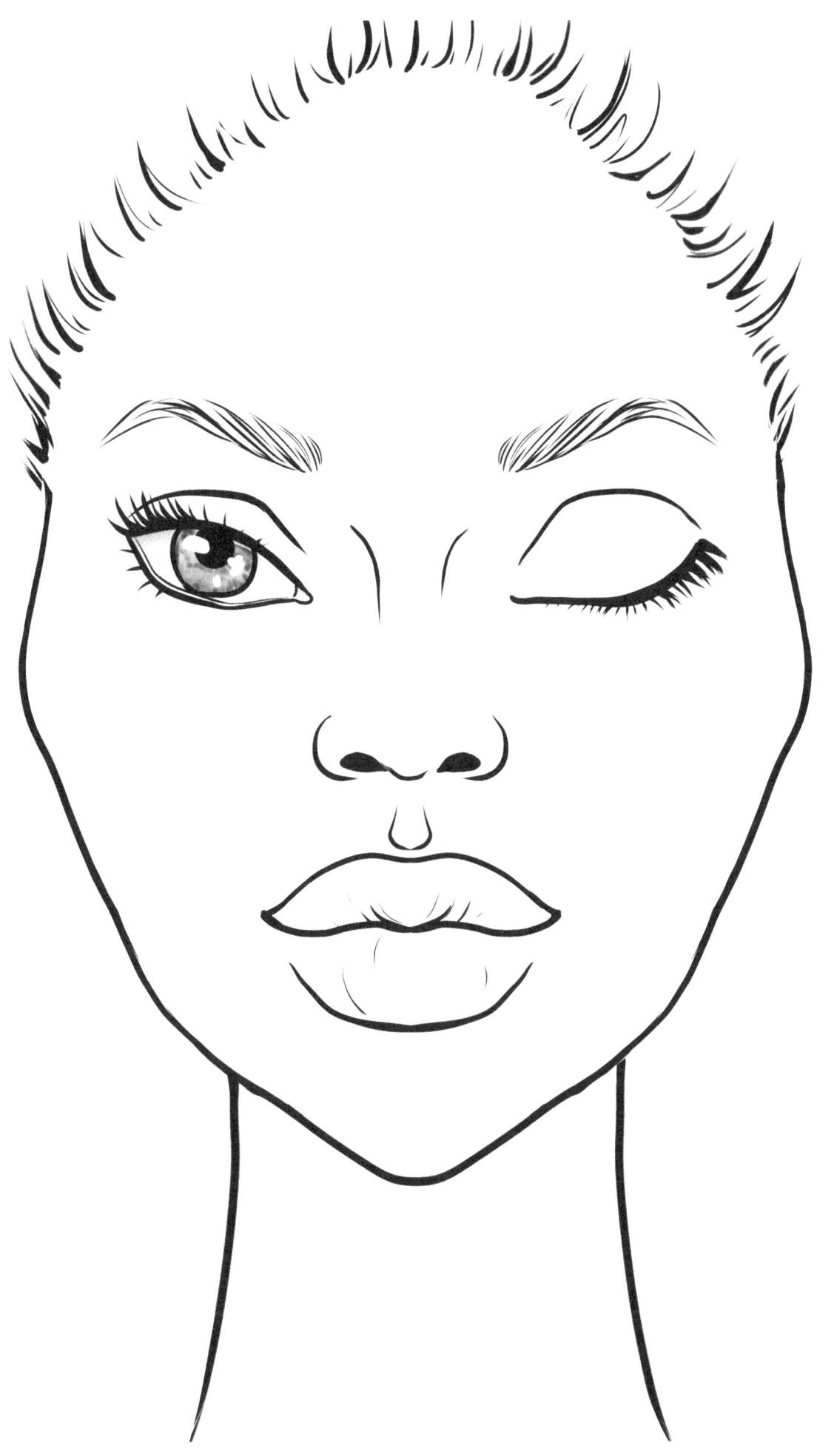

PREPARATION

Cleanser

Moisturizer

Primer

FACE

Concealer

Foundation

Powder

Highlighter

Contour

Bronzer

Blush

EYES

Eyeshadow lid

Eyeshadow crease

Eyeliner

Mascara

Lashes

Brows

LIPS

Lip color

Lip liner

Lip gloss

OTHER

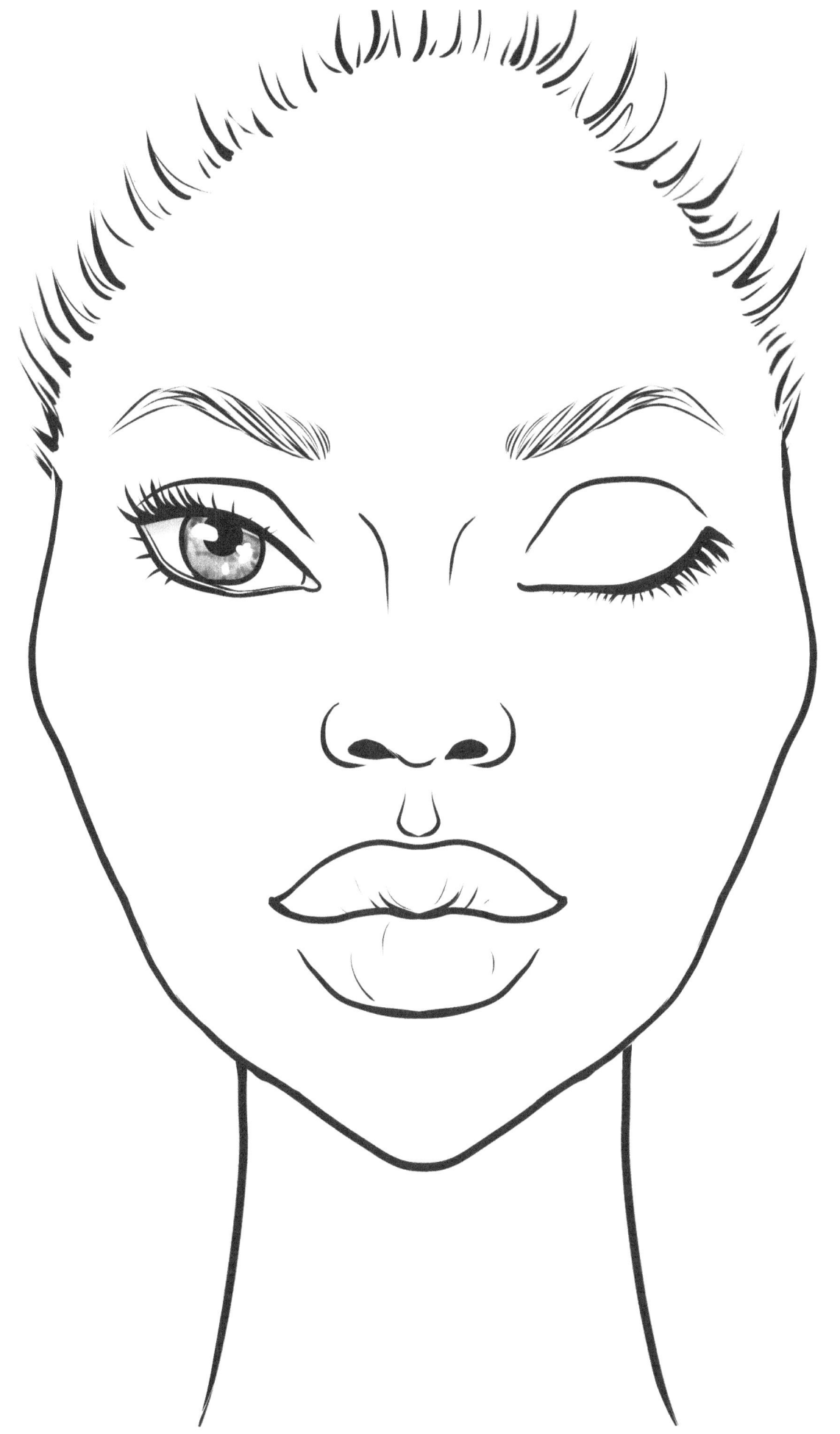

PREPARATION

Cleanser

Moisturizer

Primer

FACE

Concealer

Foundation

Powder

Highlighter

Contour

Bronzer

Blush

EYES

Eyeshadow lid

Eyeshadow crease

Eyeliner

Mascara

Lashes

Brows

LIPS

Lip color

Lip liner

Lip gloss

OTHER

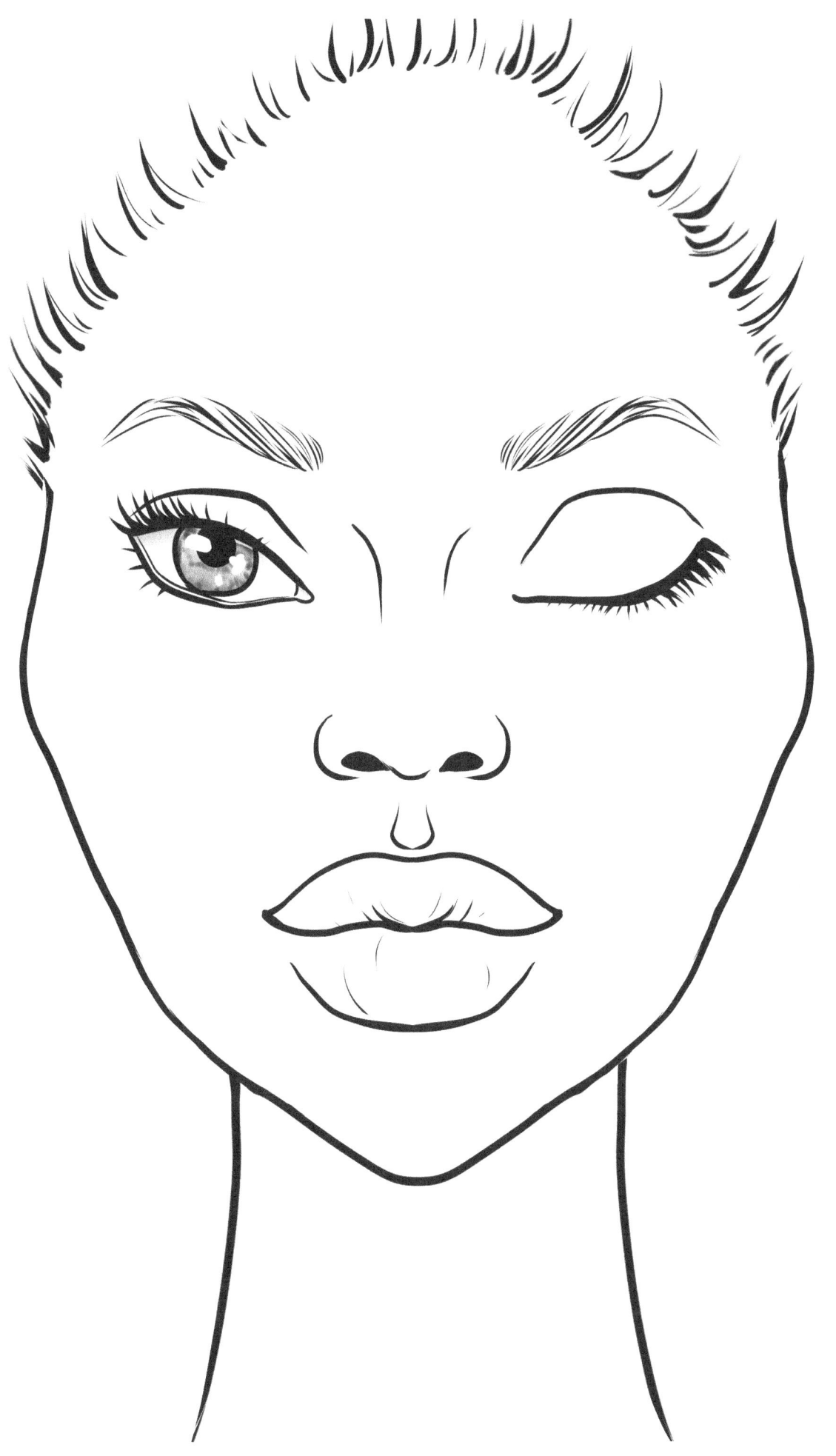

PREPARATION

Cleanser

Moisturizer

Primer

FACE

Concealer

Foundation

Powder

Highlighter

Contour

Bronzer

Blush

EYES

Eyeshadow lid

Eyeshadow crease

Eyeliner

Mascara

Lashes

Brows

LIPS

Lip color

Lip liner

Lip gloss

OTHER

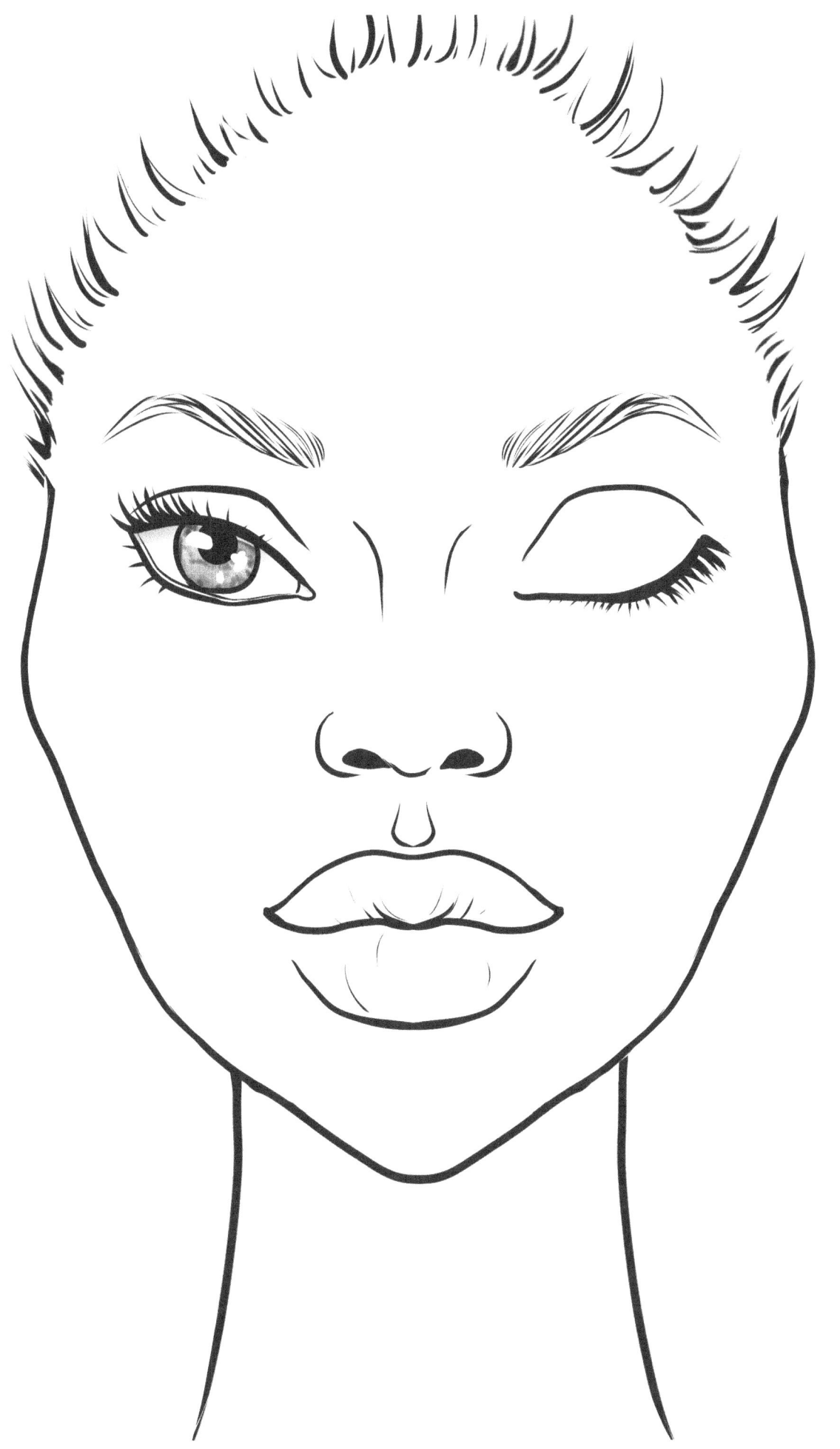

PREPARATION

Cleanser

Moisturizer

Primer

FACE

Concealer

Foundation

Powder

Highlighter

Contour

Bronzer

Blush

EYES

Eyeshadow lid

Eyeshadow crease

Eyeliner

Mascara

Lashes

Brows

LIPS

Lip color

Lip liner

Lip gloss

OTHER

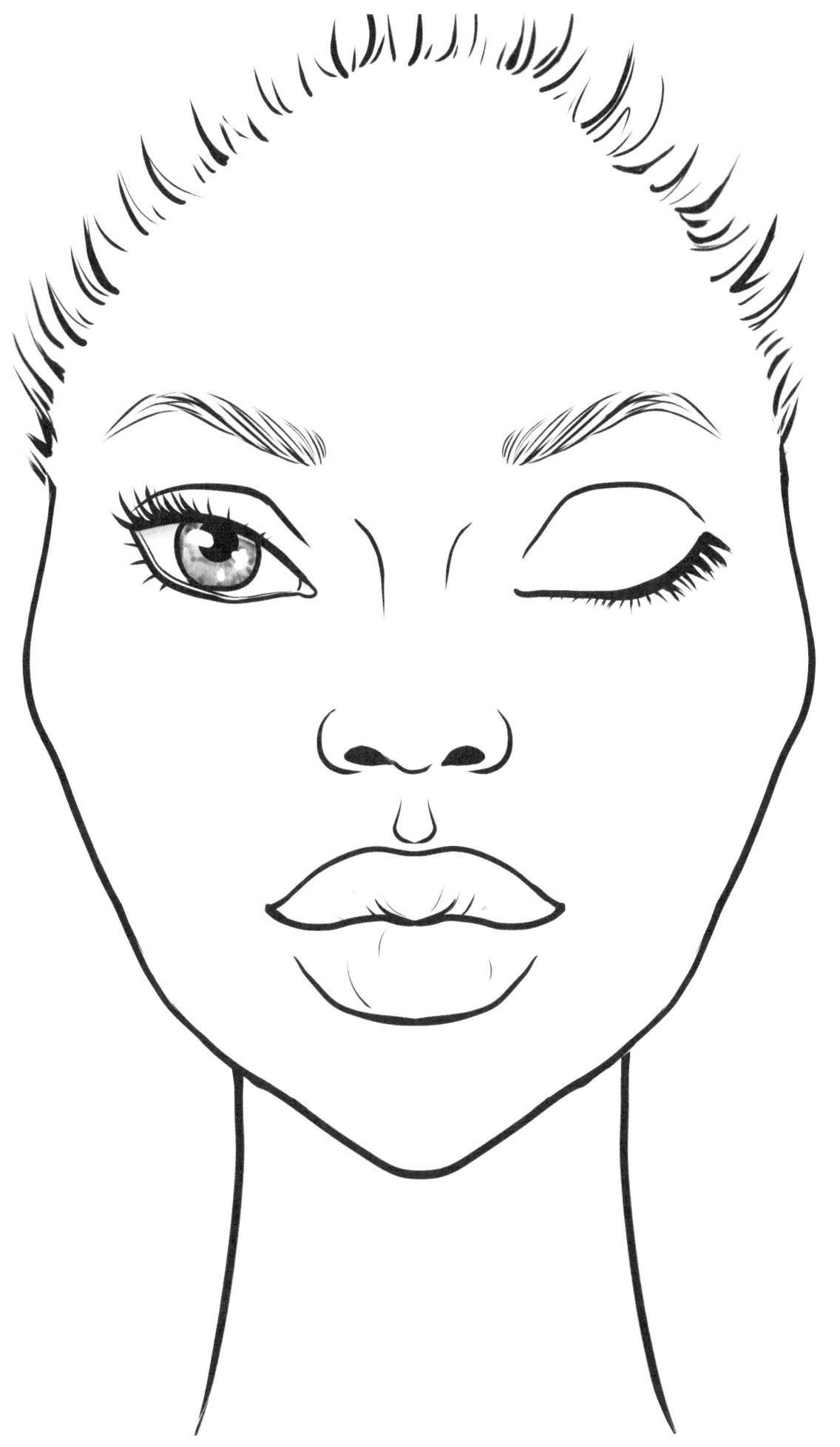

PREPARATION

Cleanser

Moisturizer

Primer

FACE

Concealer

Foundation

Powder

Highlighter

Contour

Bronzer

Blush

EYES

Eyeshadow lid

Eyeshadow crease

Eyeliner

Mascara

Lashes

Brows

LIPS

Lip color

Lip liner

Lip gloss

OTHER

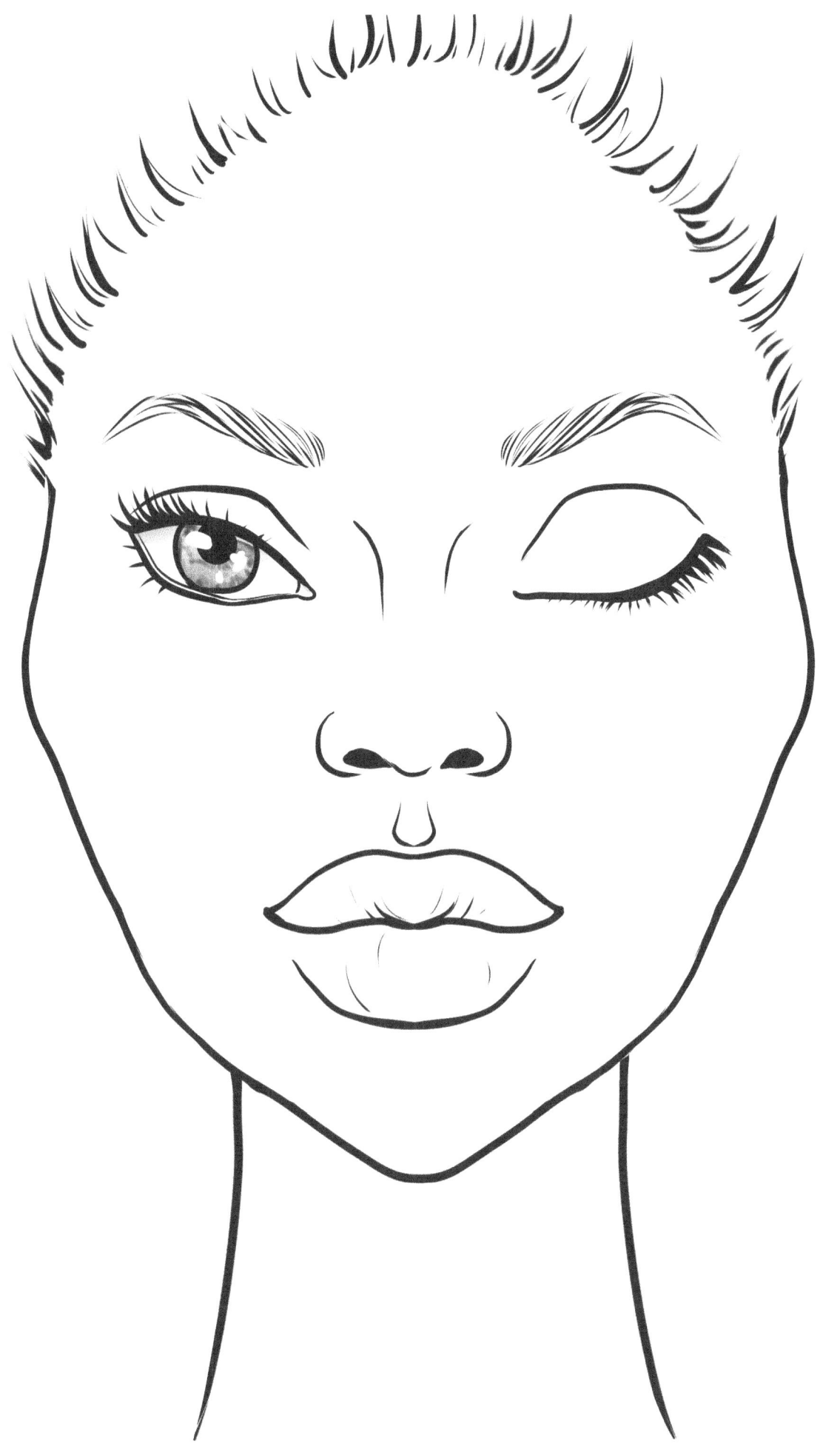

PREPARATION

Cleanser

Moisturizer

Primer

FACE

Concealer

Foundation

Powder

Highlighter

Contour

Bronzer

Blush

EYES

Eyeshadow lid

Eyeshadow crease

Eyeliner

Mascara

Lashes

Brows

LIPS

Lip color

Lip liner

Lip gloss

OTHER

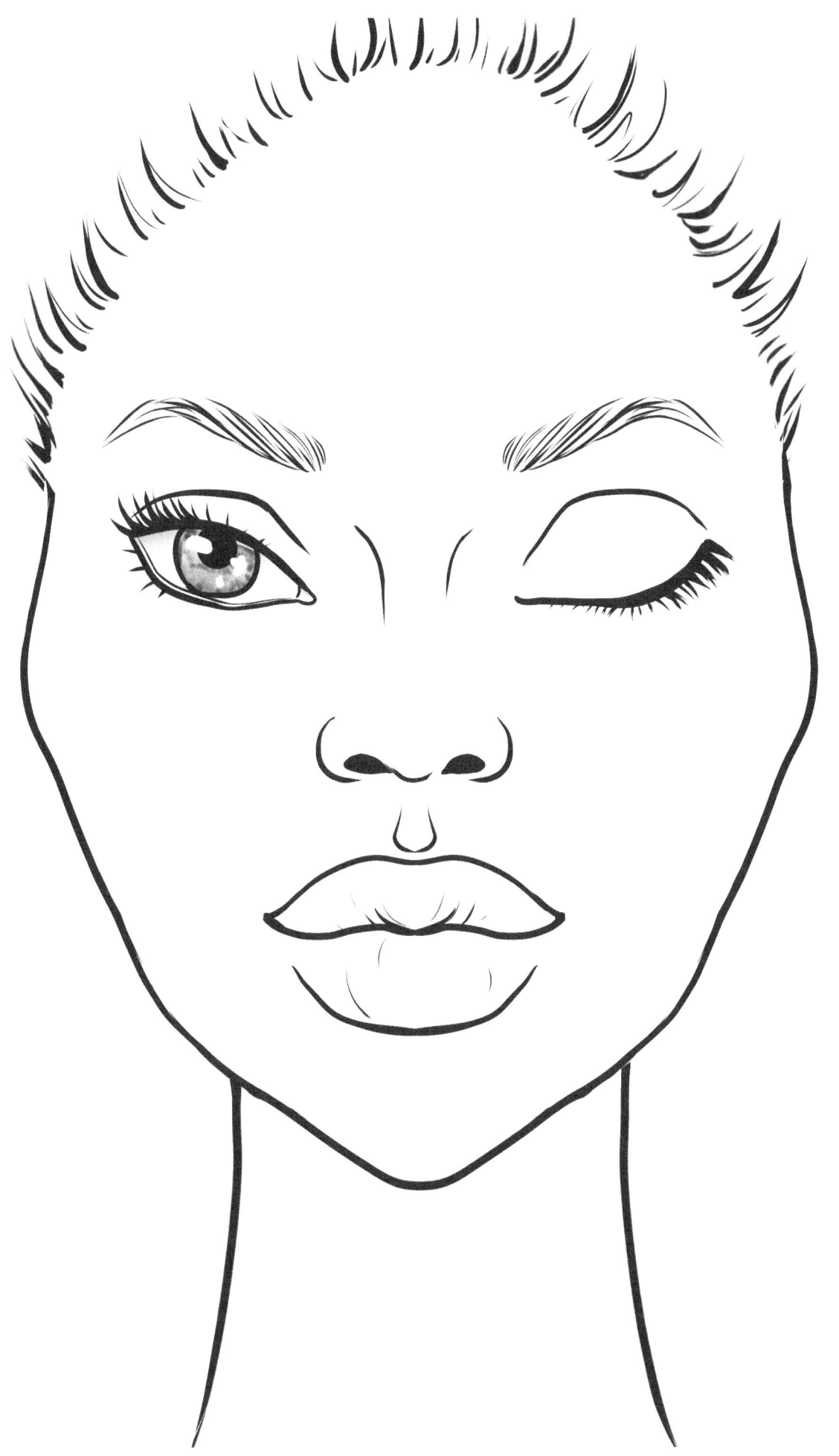

PREPARATION

Cleanser

Moisturizer

Primer

FACE

Concealer

Foundation

Powder

Highlighter

Contour

Bronzer

Blush

EYES

Eyeshadow lid

Eyeshadow crease

Eyeliner

Mascara

Lashes

Brows

LIPS

Lip color

Lip liner

Lip gloss

OTHER

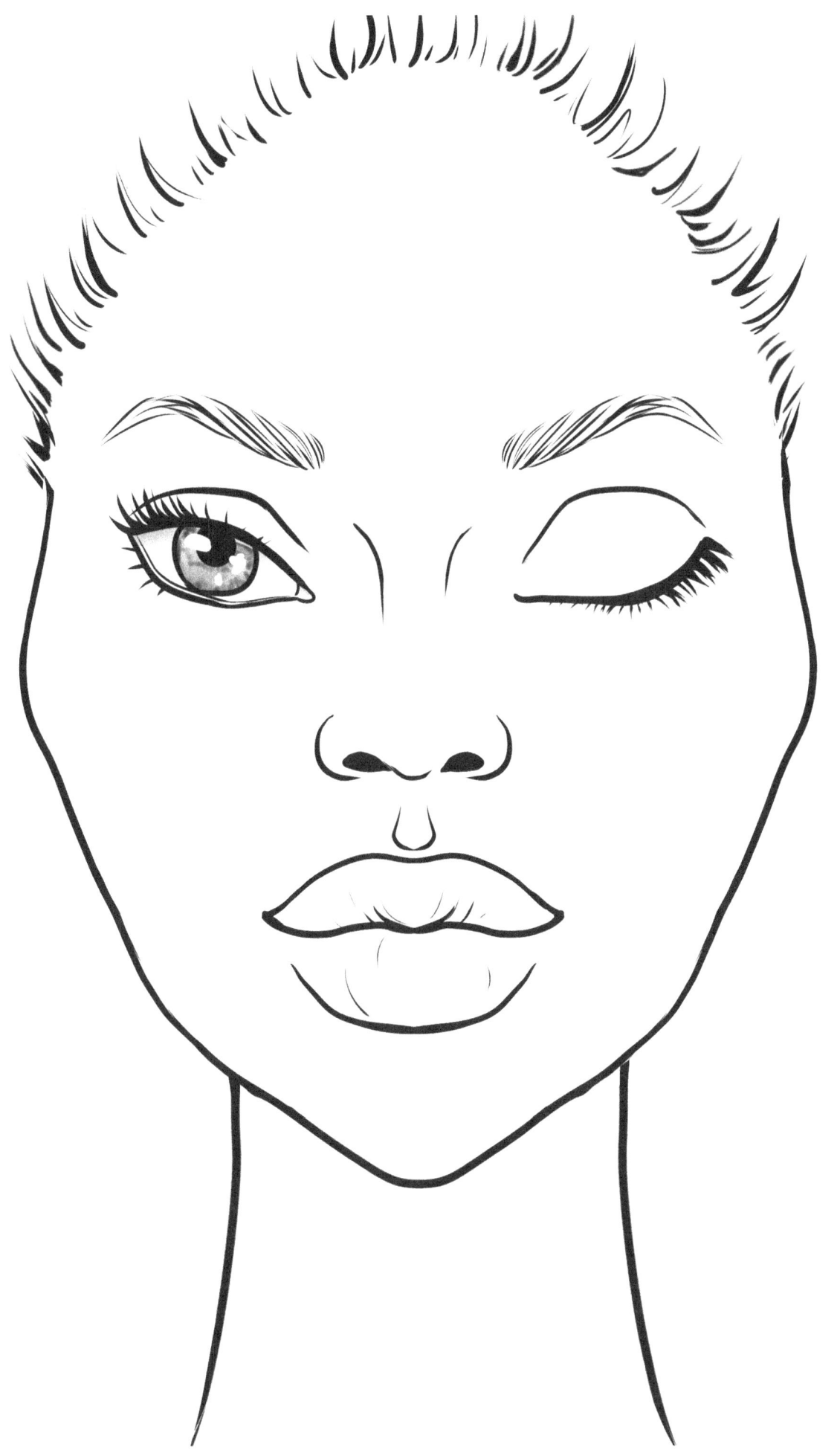

CLOSED EYES
FACE CHARTS

PREPARATION

Cleanser

Moisturizer

Primer

FACE

Concealer

Foundation

Powder

Highlighter

Contour

Bronzer

Blush

EYES

Eyeshadow lid

Eyeshadow crease

Eyeliner

Mascara

Lashes

Brows

LIPS

Lip color

Lip liner

Lip gloss

OTHER

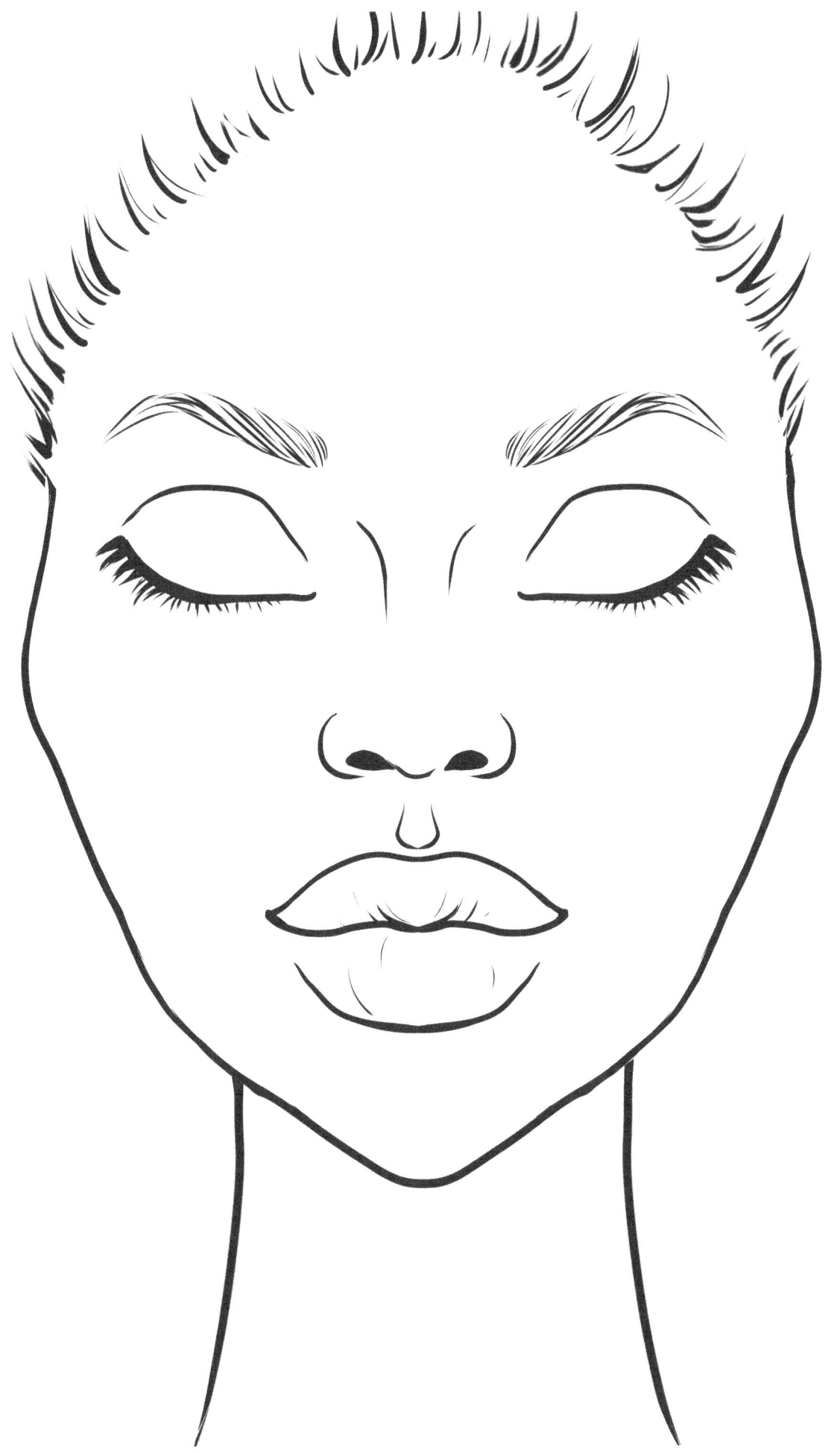

PREPARATION

Cleanser

Moisturizer

Primer

FACE

Concealer

Foundation

Powder

Highlighter

Contour

Bronzer

Blush

EYES

Eyeshadow lid

Eyeshadow crease

Eyeliner

Mascara

Lashes

Brows

LIPS

Lip color

Lip liner

Lip gloss

OTHER

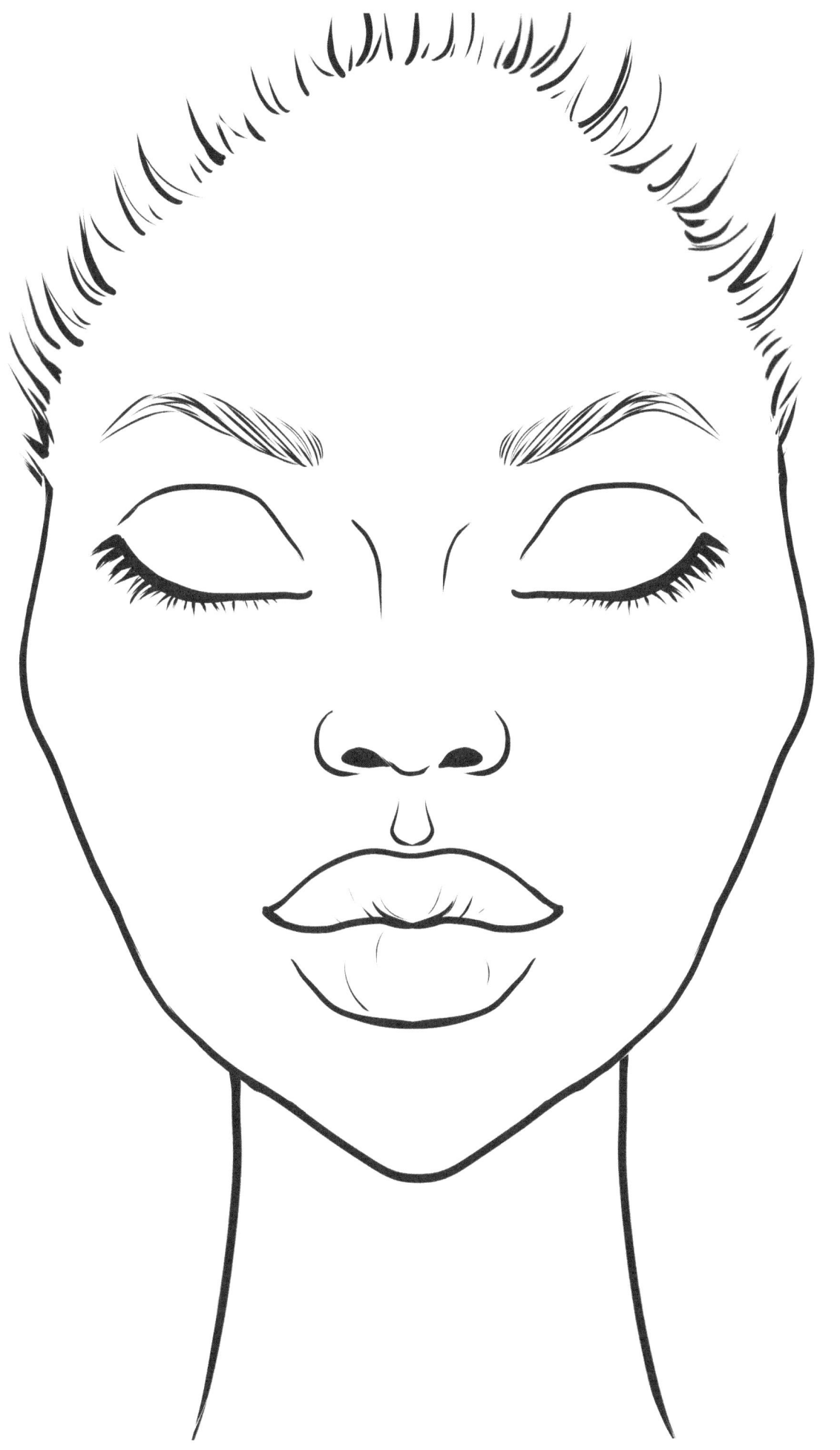

PREPARATION

Cleanser

Moisturizer

Primer

FACE

Concealer

Foundation

Powder

Highlighter

Contour

Bronzer

Blush

EYES

Eyeshadow lid

Eyeshadow crease

Eyeliner

Mascara

Lashes

Brows

LIPS

Lip color

Lip liner

Lip gloss

OTHER

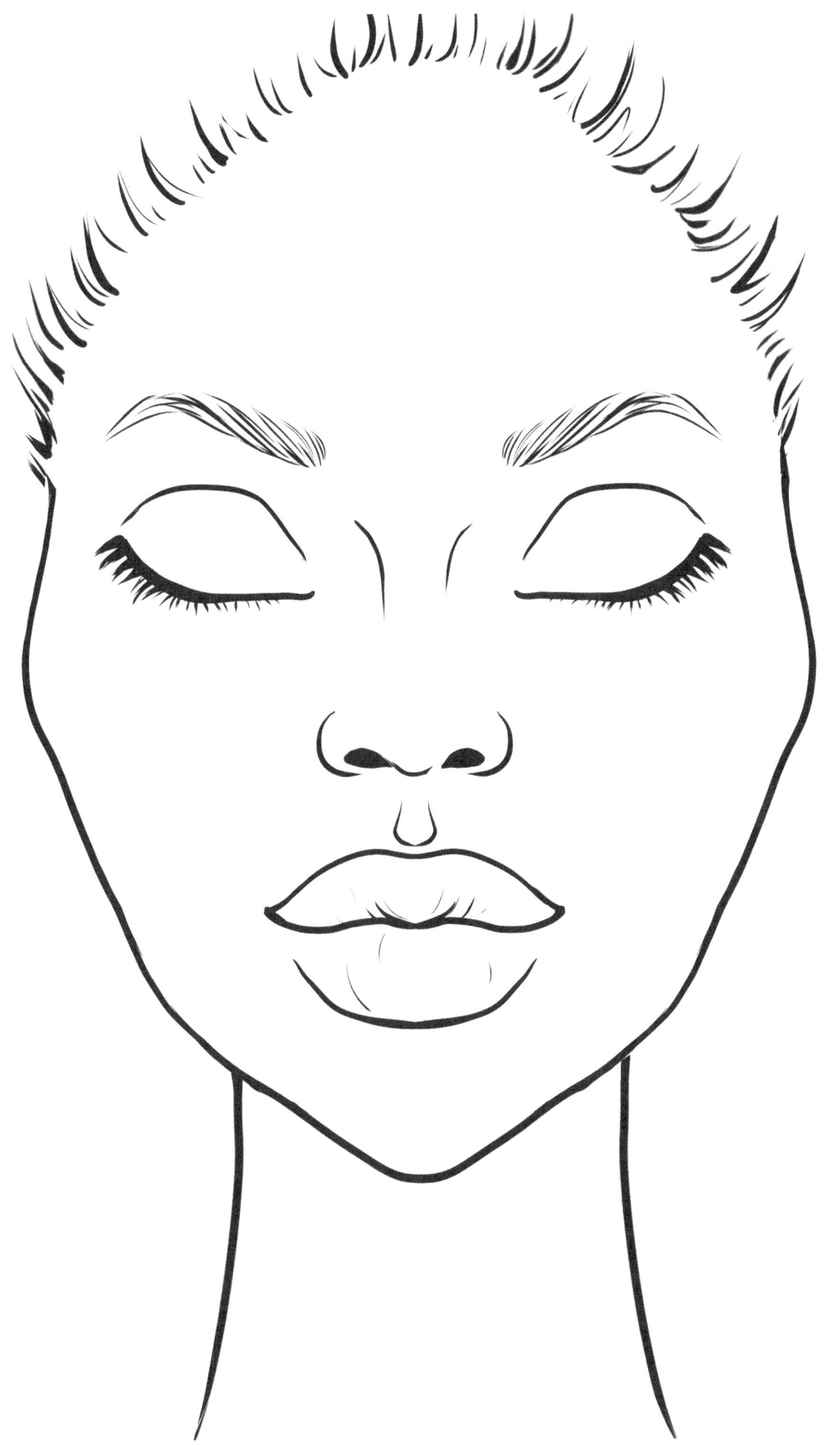

PREPARATION

Cleanser

Moisturizer

Primer

FACE

Concealer

Foundation

Powder

Highlighter

Contour

Bronzer

Blush

EYES

Eyeshadow lid

Eyeshadow crease

Eyeliner

Mascara

Lashes

Brows

LIPS

Lip color

Lip liner

Lip gloss

OTHER

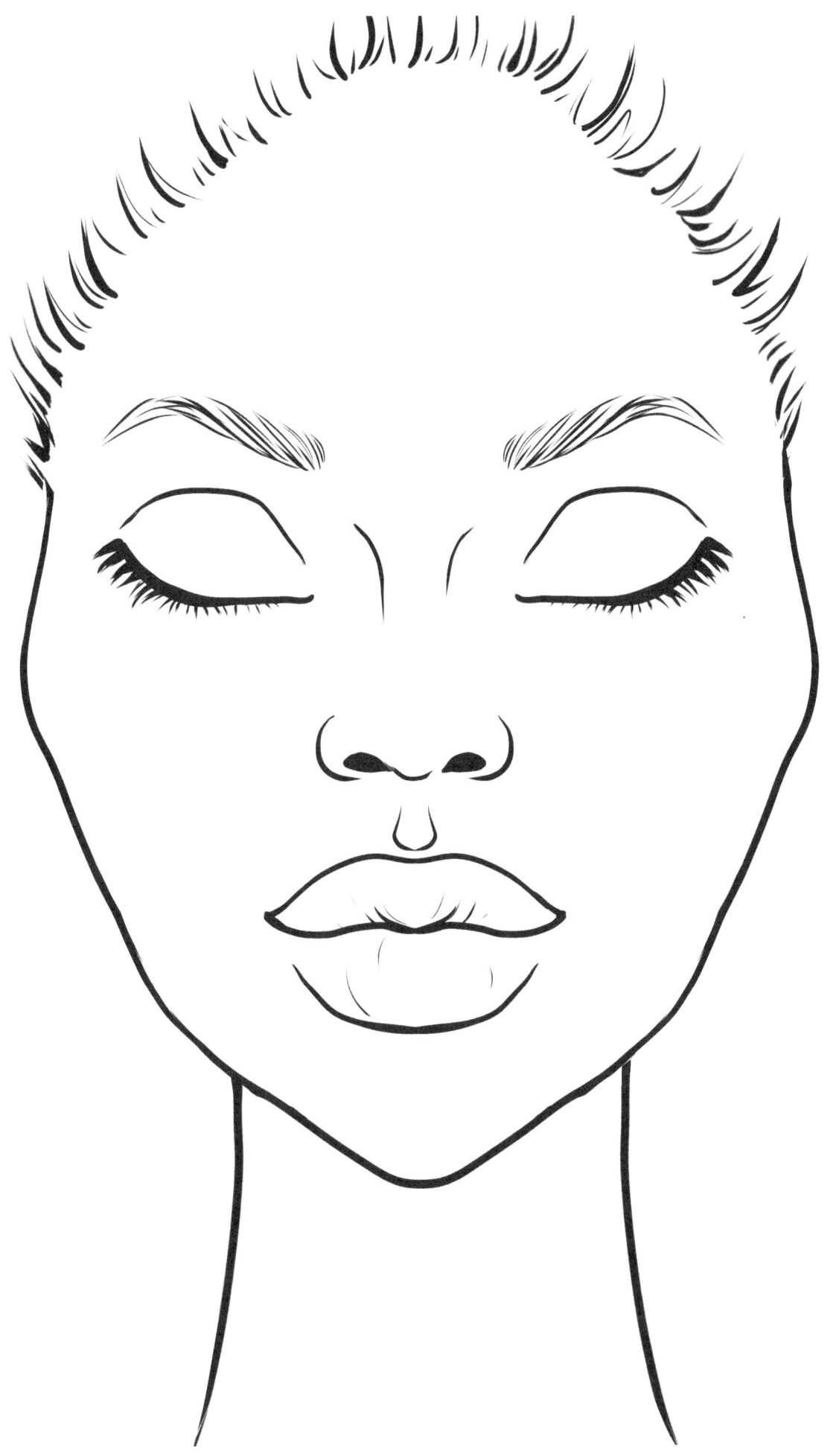

PREPARATION

Cleanser

Moisturizer

Primer

FACE

Concealer

Foundation

Powder

Highlighter

Contour

Bronzer

Blush

EYES

Eyeshadow lid

Eyeshadow crease

Eyeliner

Mascara

Lashes

Brows

LIPS

Lip color

Lip liner

Lip gloss

OTHER

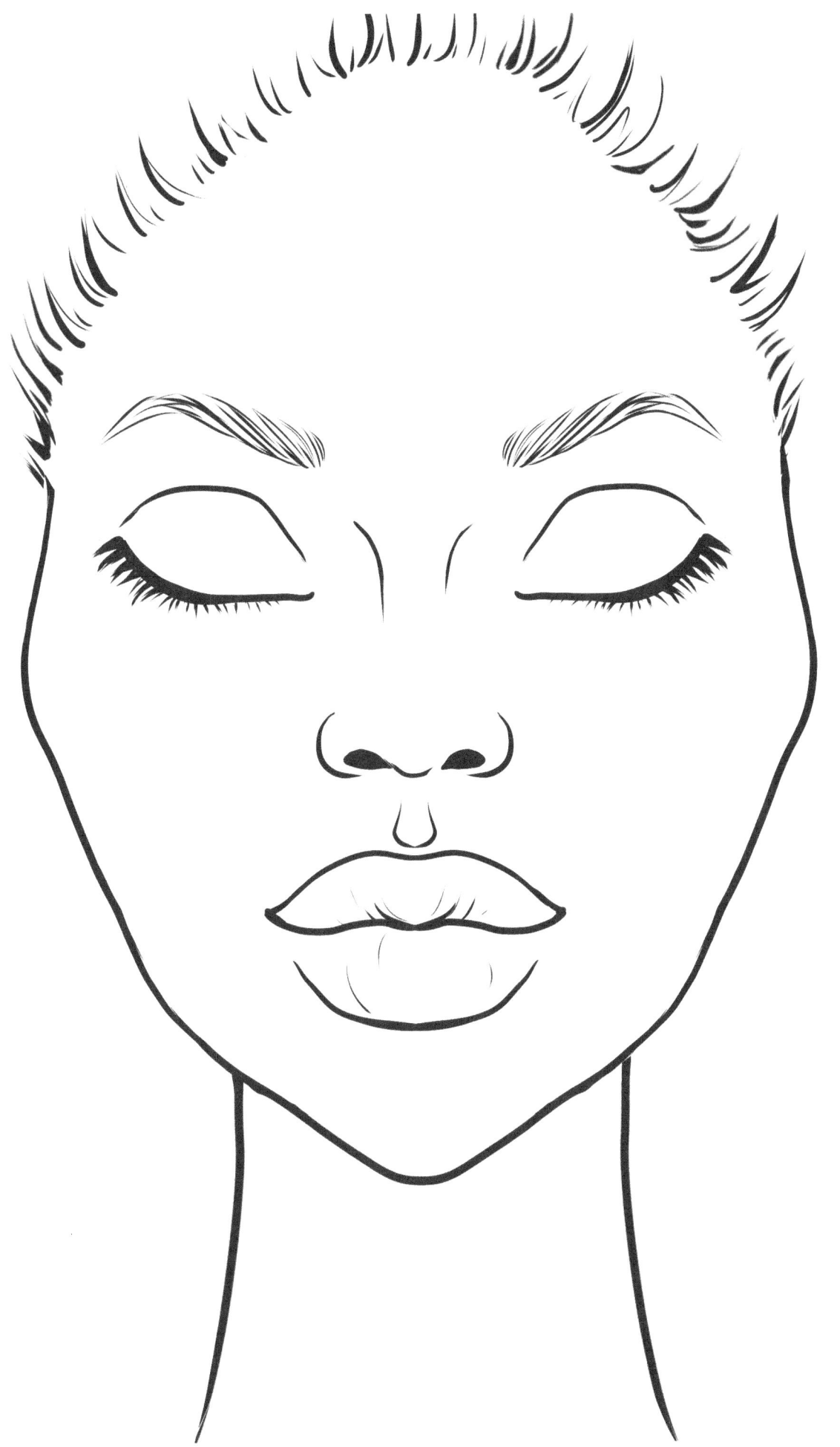

PREPARATION

Cleanser

Moisturizer

Primer

FACE

Concealer

Foundation

Powder

Highlighter

Contour

Bronzer

Blush

EYES

Eyeshadow lid

Eyeshadow crease

Eyeliner

Mascara

Lashes

Brows

LIPS

Lip color

Lip liner

Lip gloss

OTHER

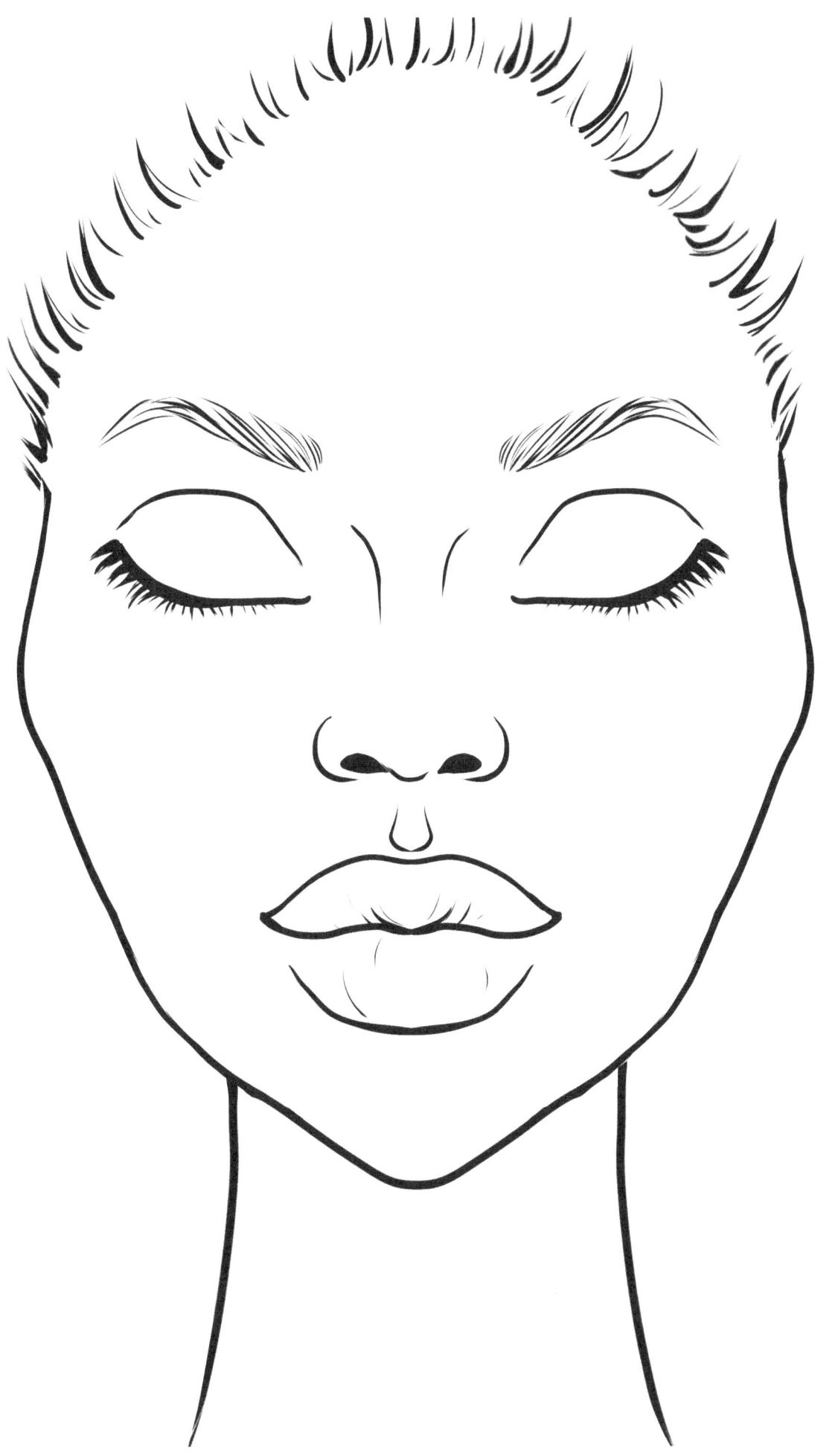

PREPARATION

Cleanser

Moisturizer

Primer

FACE

Concealer

Foundation

Powder

Highlighter

Contour

Bronzer

Blush

EYES

Eyeshadow lid

Eyeshadow crease

Eyeliner

Mascara

Lashes

Brows

LIPS

Lip color

Lip liner

Lip gloss

OTHER

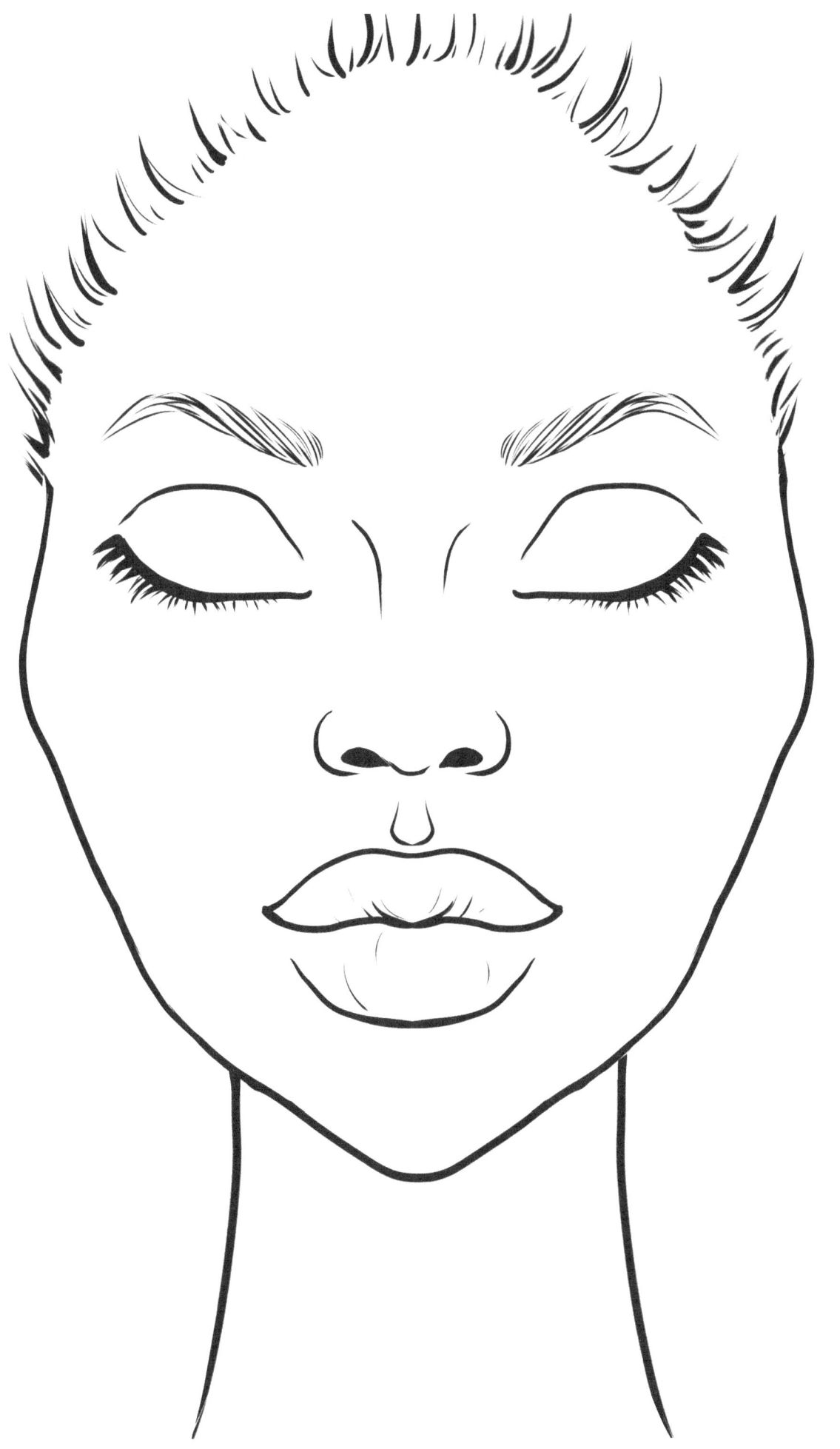

PREPARATION

Cleanser

Moisturizer

Primer

FACE

Concealer

Foundation

Powder

Highlighter

Contour

Bronzer

Blush

EYES

Eyeshadow lid

Eyeshadow crease

Eyeliner

Mascara

Lashes

Brows

LIPS

Lip color

Lip liner

Lip gloss

OTHER

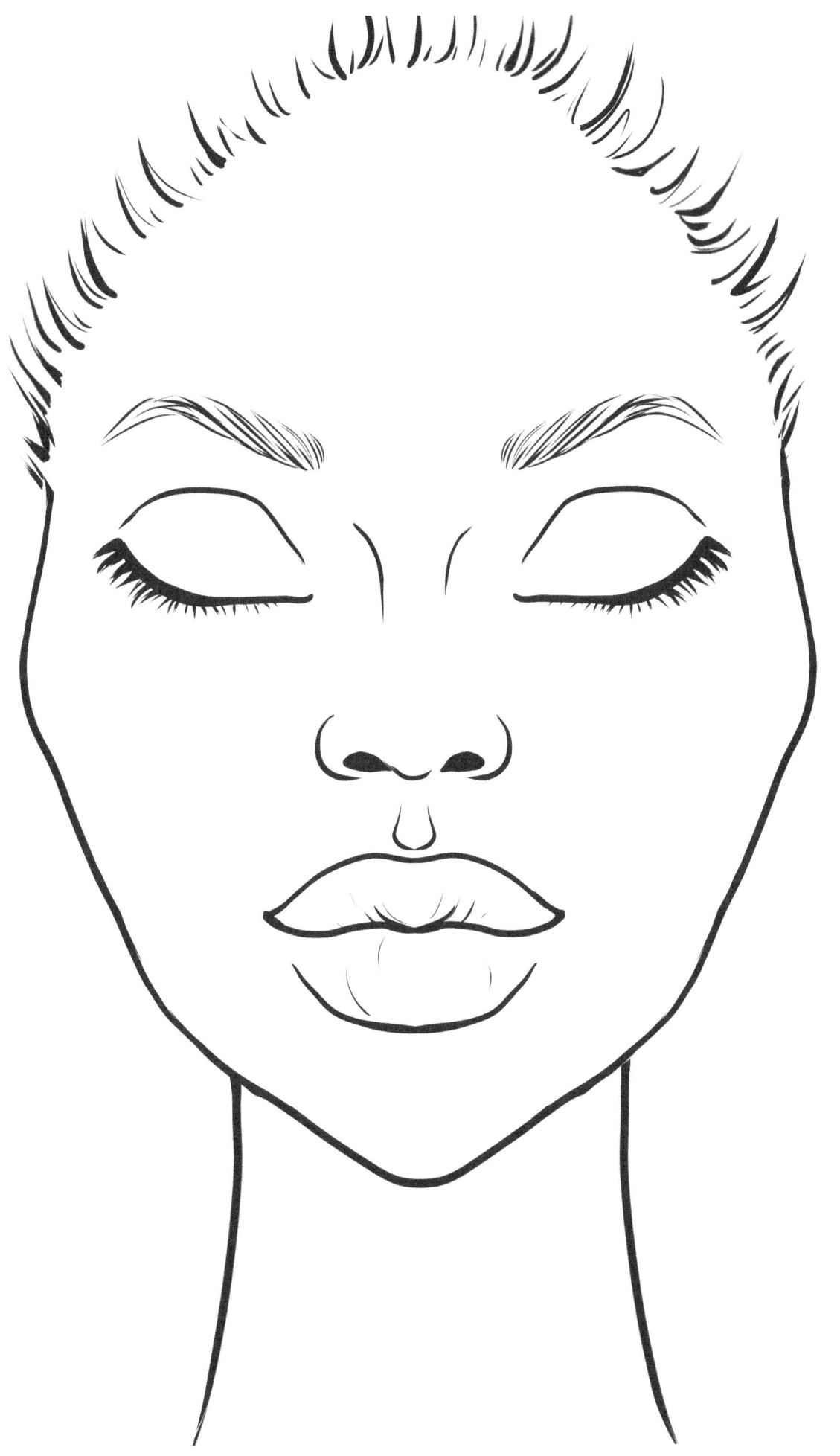

PREPARATION

Cleanser

Moisturizer

Primer

FACE

Concealer

Foundation

Powder

Highlighter

Contour

Bronzer

Blush

EYES

Eyeshadow lid

Eyeshadow crease

Eyeliner

Mascara

Lashes

Brows

LIPS

Lip color

Lip liner

Lip gloss

OTHER

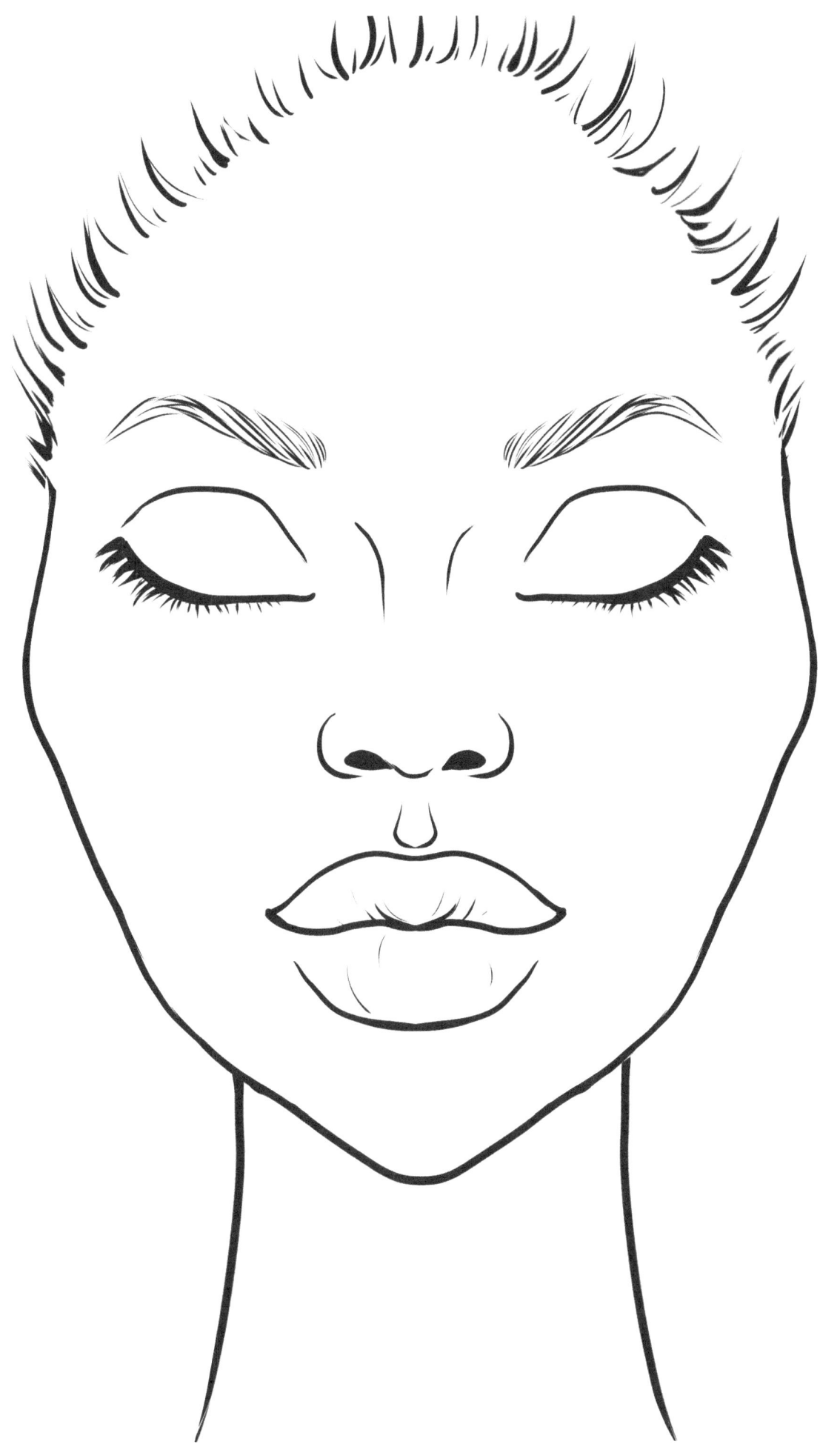

PREPARATION

Cleanser

Moisturizer

Primer

FACE

Concealer

Foundation

Powder

Highlighter

Contour

Bronzer

Blush

EYES

Eyeshadow lid

Eyeshadow crease

Eyeliner

Mascara

Lashes

Brows

LIPS

Lip color

Lip liner

Lip gloss

OTHER

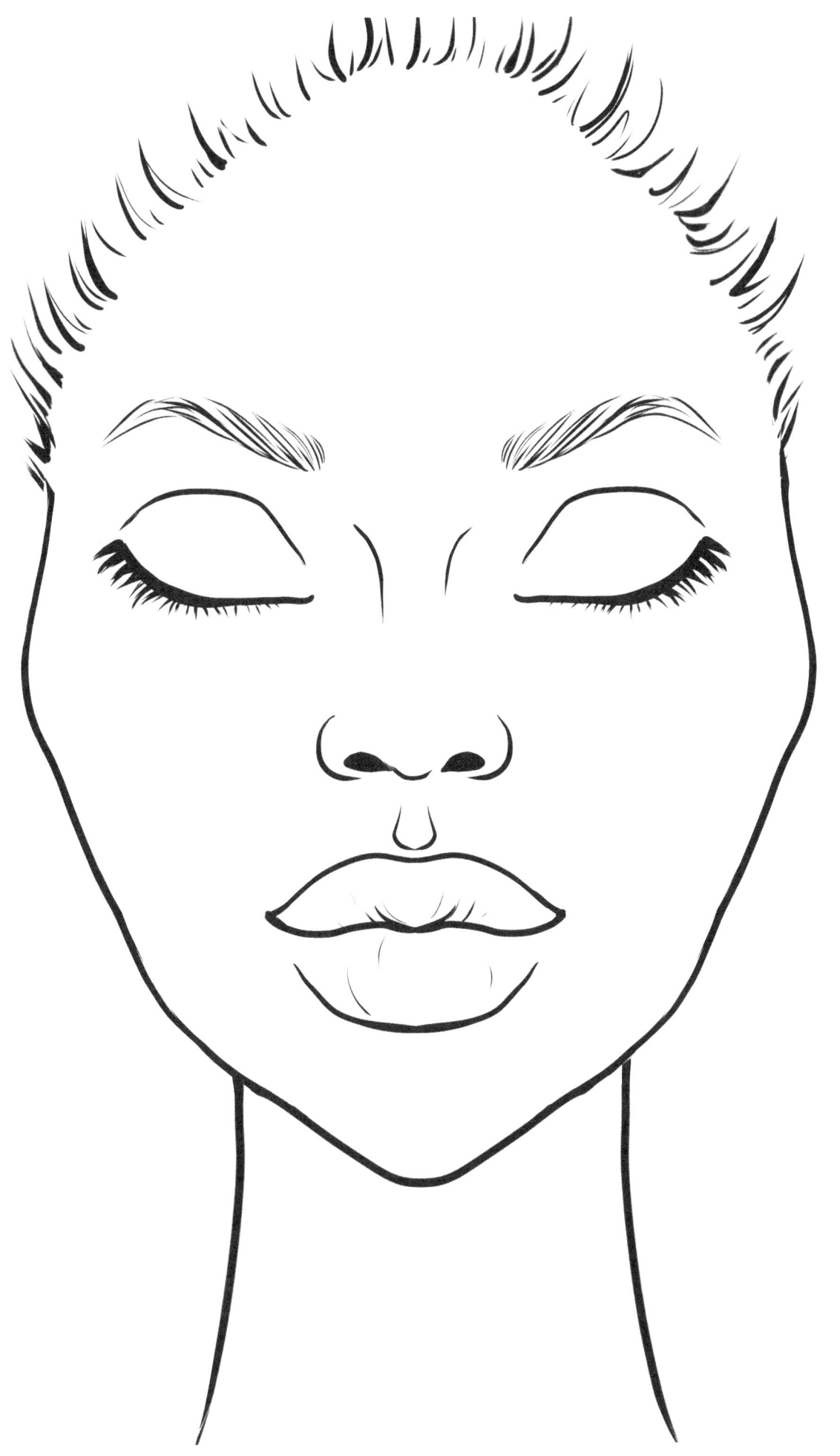

PREPARATION

Cleanser

Moisturizer

Primer

FACE

Concealer

Foundation

Powder

Highlighter

Contour

Bronzer

Blush

EYES

Eyeshadow lid

Eyeshadow crease

Eyeliner

Mascara

Lashes

Brows

LIPS

Lip color

Lip liner

Lip gloss

OTHER

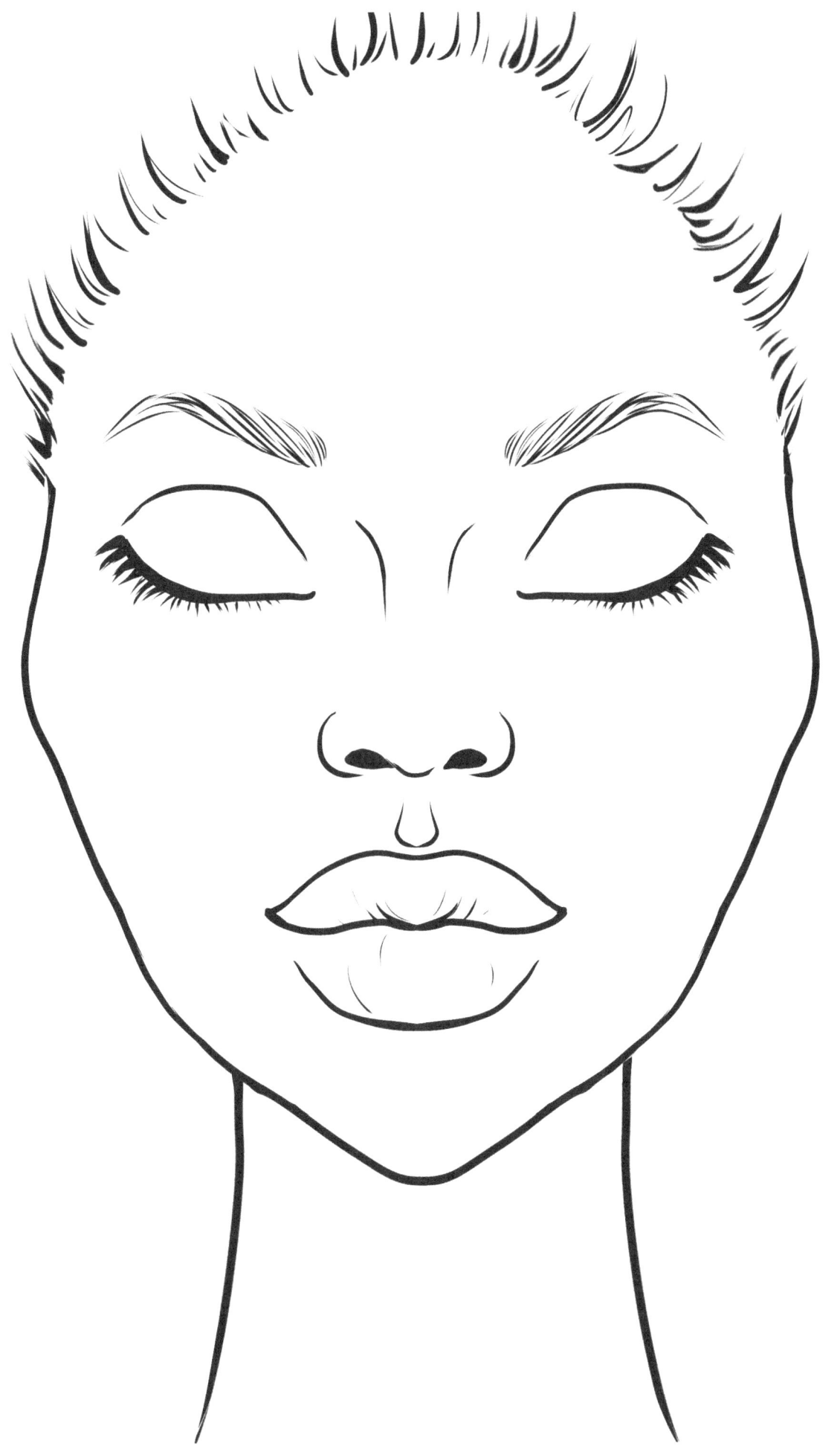

PREPARATION

Cleanser

Moisturizer

Primer

FACE

Concealer

Foundation

Powder

Highlighter

Contour

Bronzer

Blush

EYES

Eyeshadow lid

Eyeshadow crease

Eyeliner

Mascara

Lashes

Brows

LIPS

Lip color

Lip liner

Lip gloss

OTHER

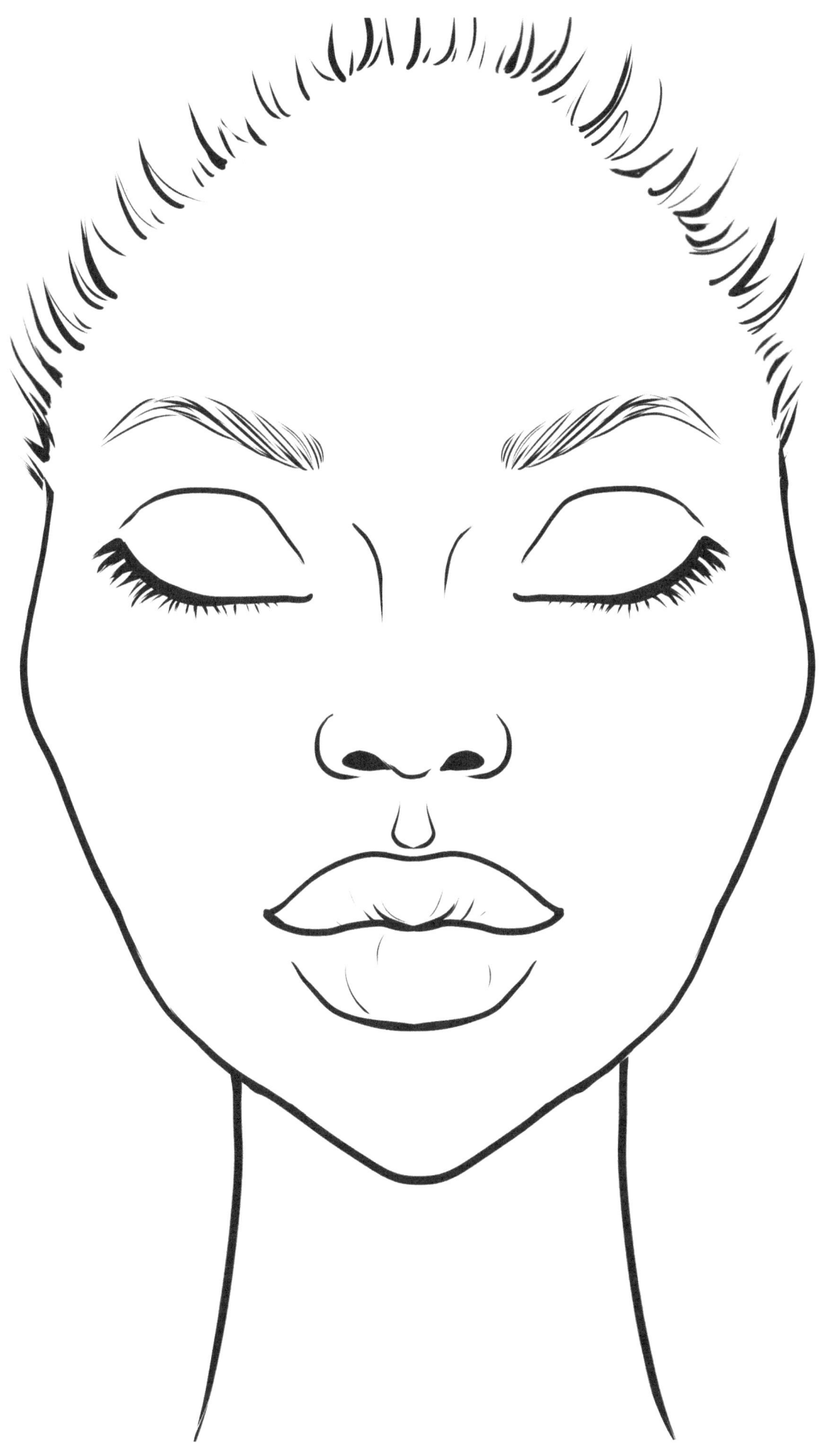

PREPARATION

Cleanser

Moisturizer

Primer

FACE

Concealer

Foundation

Powder

Highlighter

Contour

Bronzer

Blush

EYES

Eyeshadow lid

Eyeshadow crease

Eyeliner

Mascara

Lashes

Brows

LIPS

Lip color

Lip liner

Lip gloss

OTHER

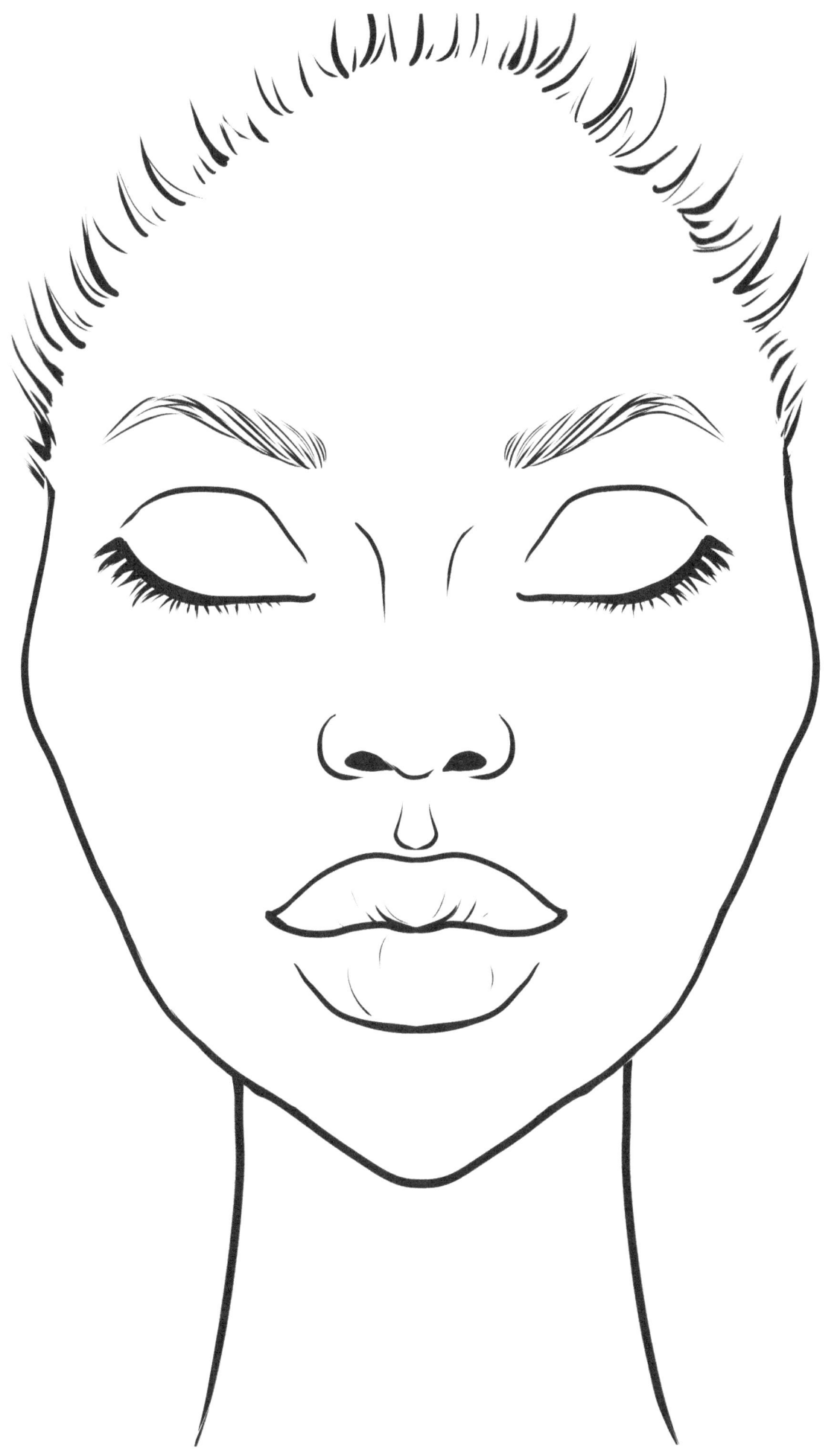

PREPARATION

Cleanser

Moisturizer

Primer

FACE

Concealer

Foundation

Powder

Highlighter

Contour

Bronzer

Blush

EYES

Eyeshadow lid

Eyeshadow crease

Eyeliner

Mascara

Lashes

Brows

LIPS

Lip color

Lip liner

Lip gloss

OTHER

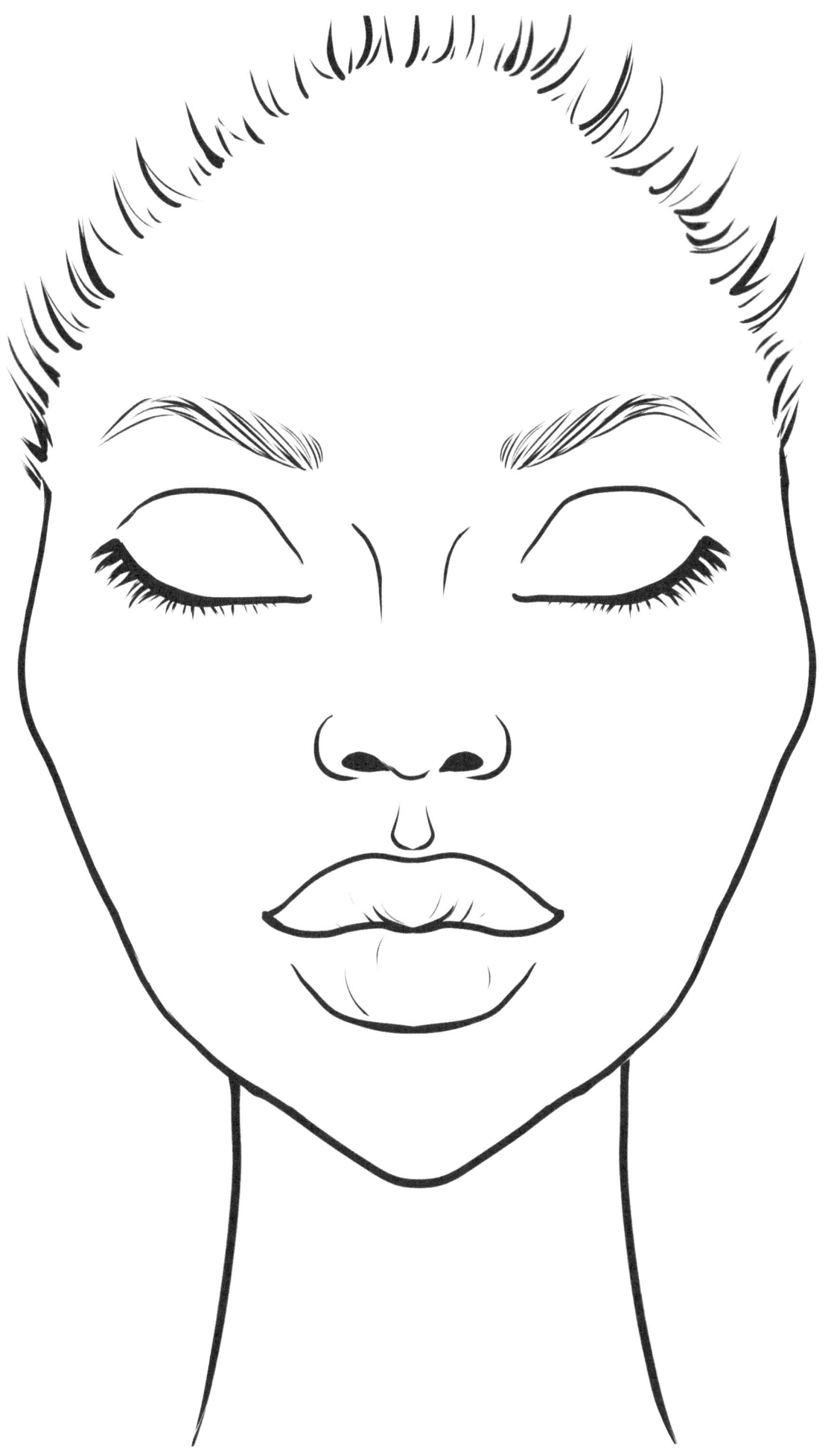

PREPARATION

Cleanser

Moisturizer

Primer

FACE

Concealer

Foundation

Powder

Highlighter

Contour

Bronzer

Blush

EYES

Eyeshadow lid

Eyeshadow crease

Eyeliner

Mascara

Lashes

Brows

LIPS

Lip color

Lip liner

Lip gloss

OTHER

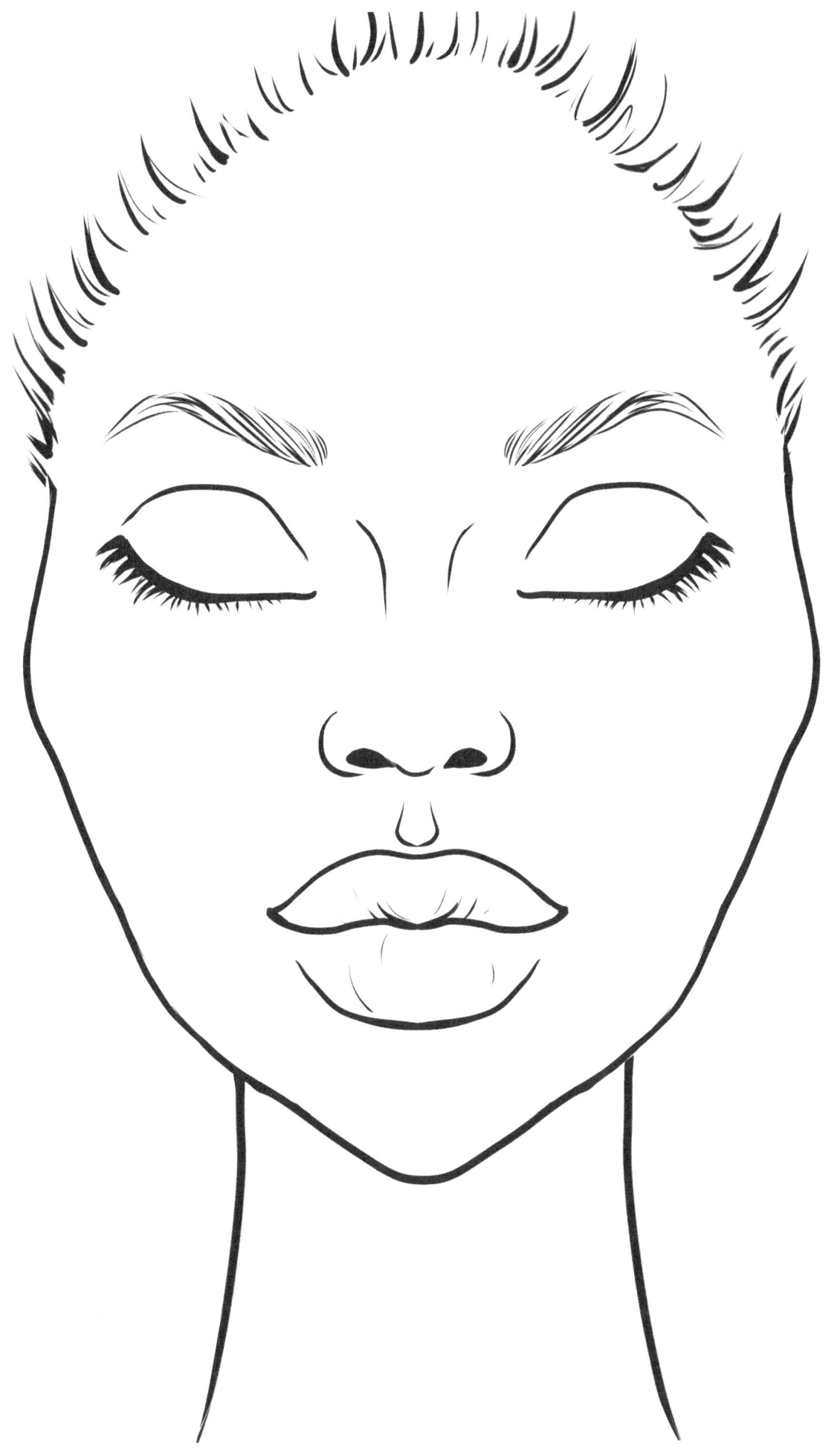

PREPARATION

Cleanser

Moisturizer

Primer

FACE

Concealer

Foundation

Powder

Highlighter

Contour

Bronzer

Blush

EYES

Eyeshadow lid

Eyeshadow crease

Eyeliner

Mascara

Lashes

Brows

LIPS

Lip color

Lip liner

Lip gloss

OTHER

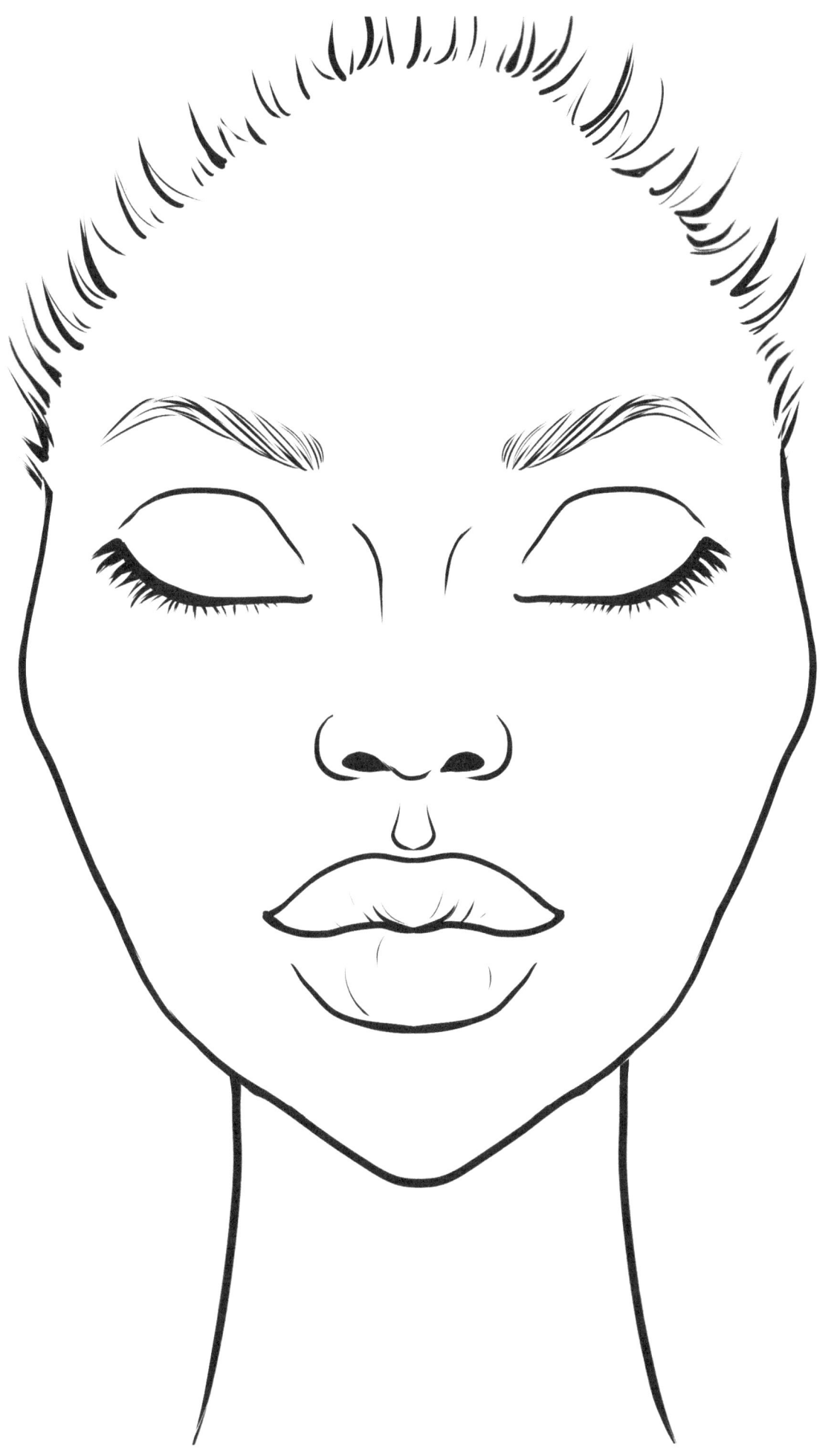

PREPARATION

Cleanser
_____

Moisturizer
_____

Primer
_____

FACE

Concealer
_____

Foundation
_____

Powder
_____

Highlighter
_____

Contour
_____

Bronzer
_____

Blush
_____

EYES

Eyeshadow lid
_____

Eyeshadow crease
_____

Eyeliner
_____

Mascara
_____

Lashes
_____

Brows
_____

LIPS

Lip color
_____

Lip liner
_____

Lip gloss

_____

OTHER

_____

_____

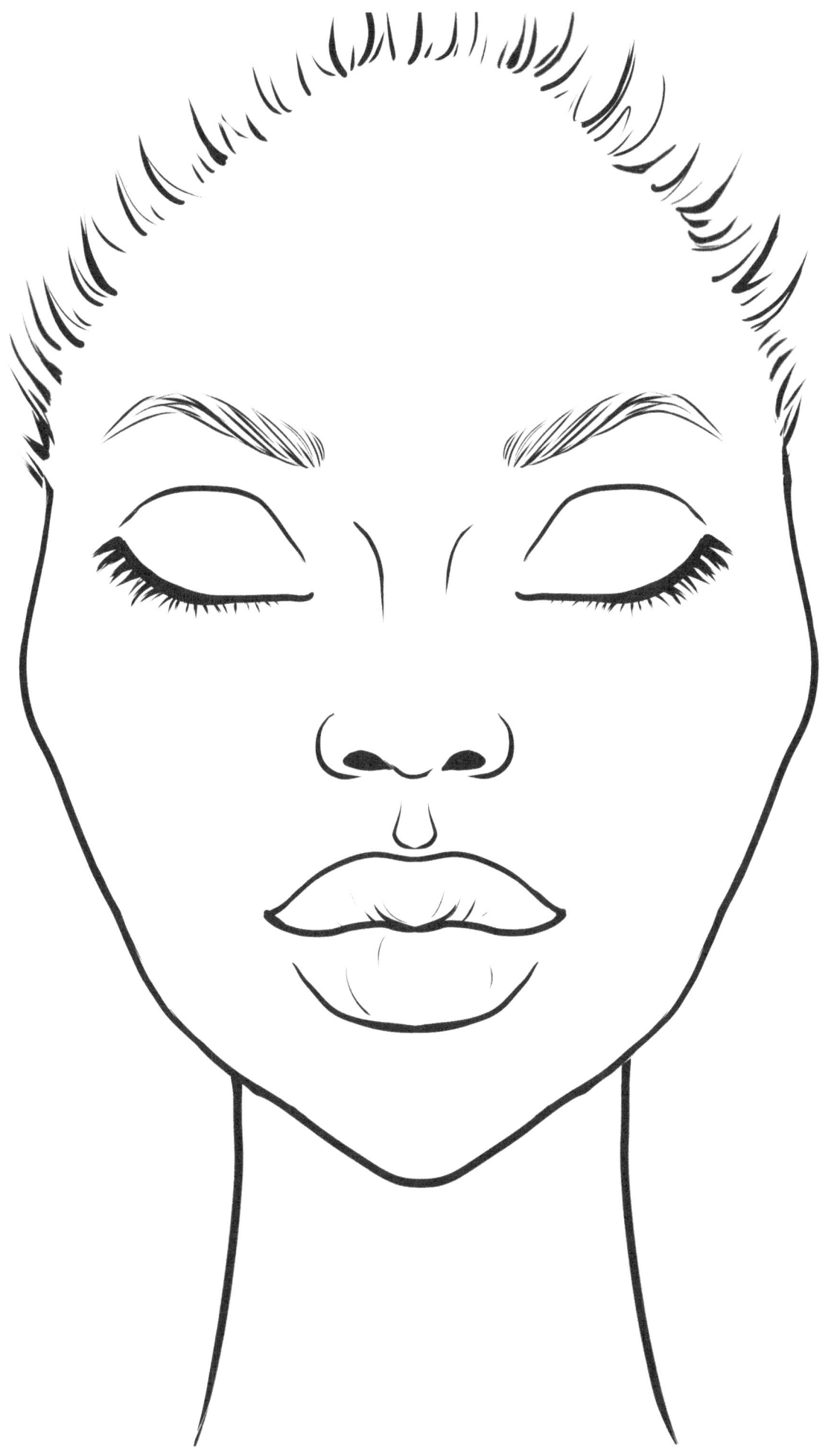

PREPARATION

Cleanser

Moisturizer

Primer

FACE

Concealer

Foundation

Powder

Highlighter

Contour

Bronzer

Blush

EYES

Eyeshadow lid

Eyeshadow crease

Eyeliner

Mascara

Lashes

Brows

LIPS

Lip color

Lip liner

Lip gloss

OTHER

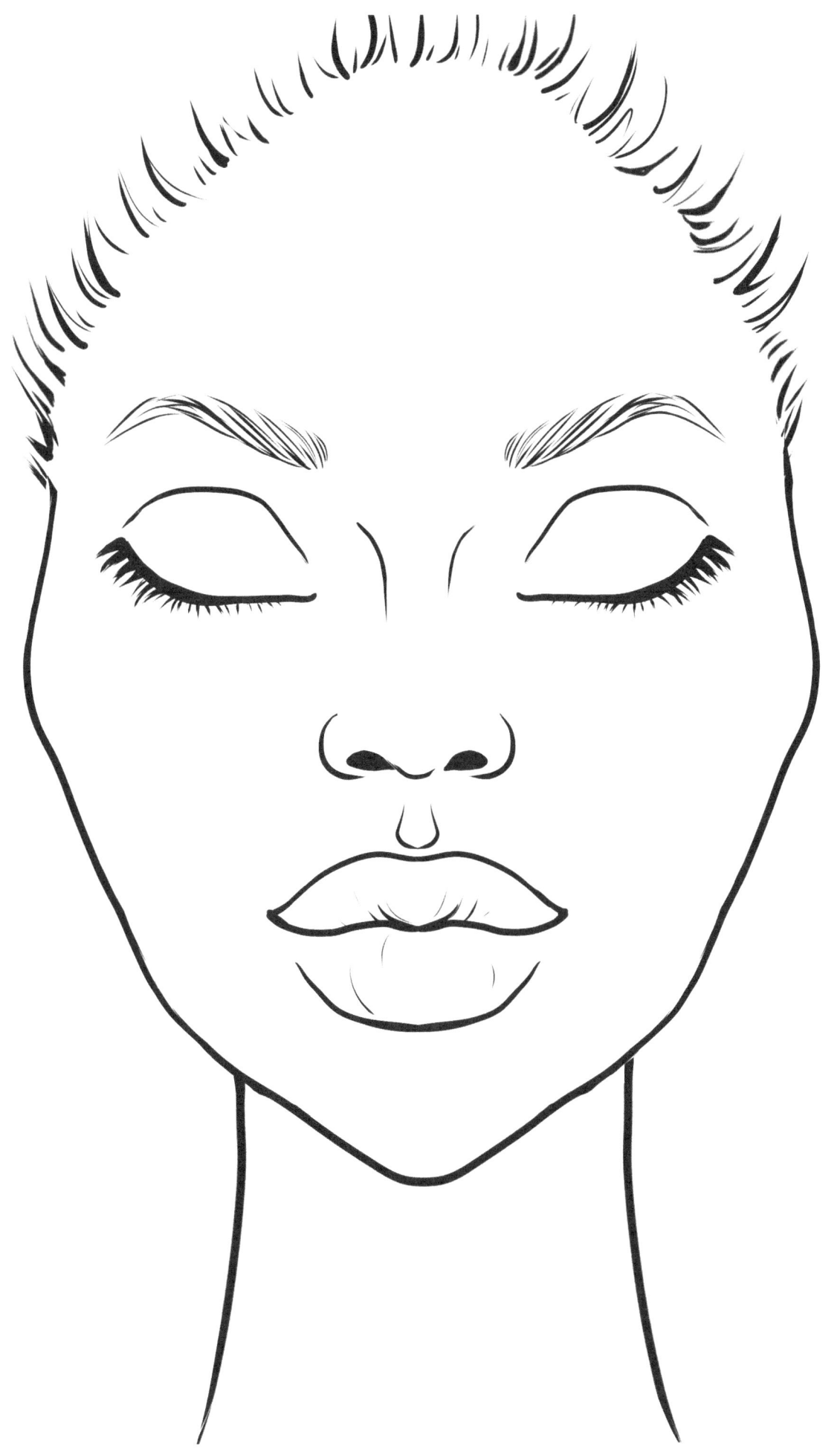

DOWNLOAD FASHION CROQUIS:

WWW.IFASHIONTEMPLATES.COM

FREE STEP-BY-STEP FASHION
DRAWING TUTORIALS:

WWW.IDRAWFASHION.COM

FASHION DESIGNING COURSES:

WWW.ACADEMY.IDRAWFASHION.COM

MORE FROM US:

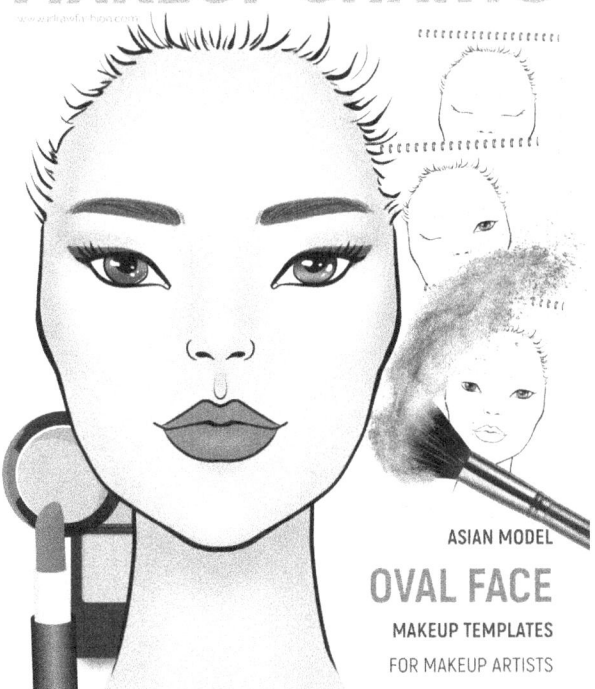

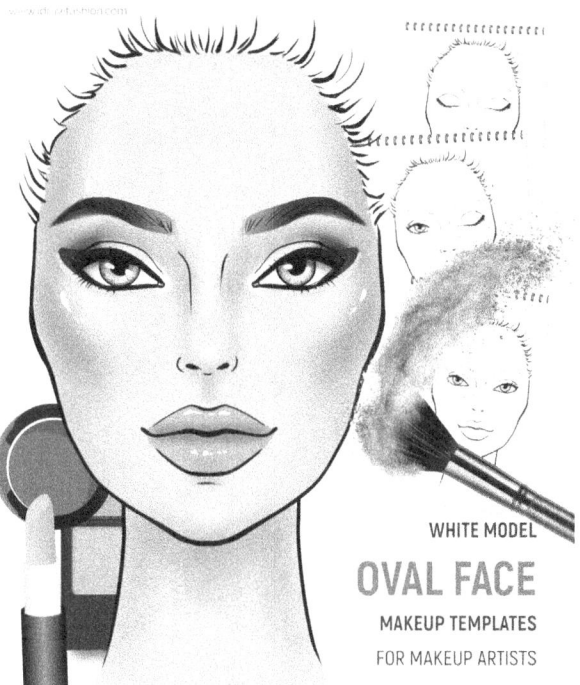

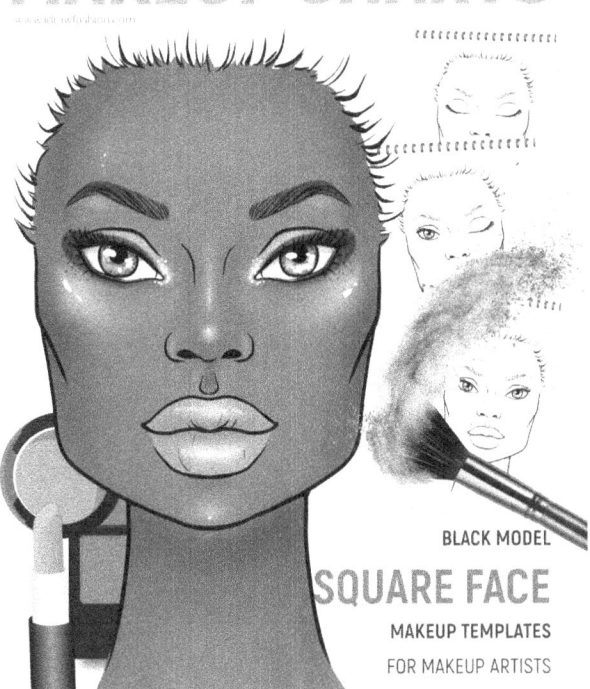

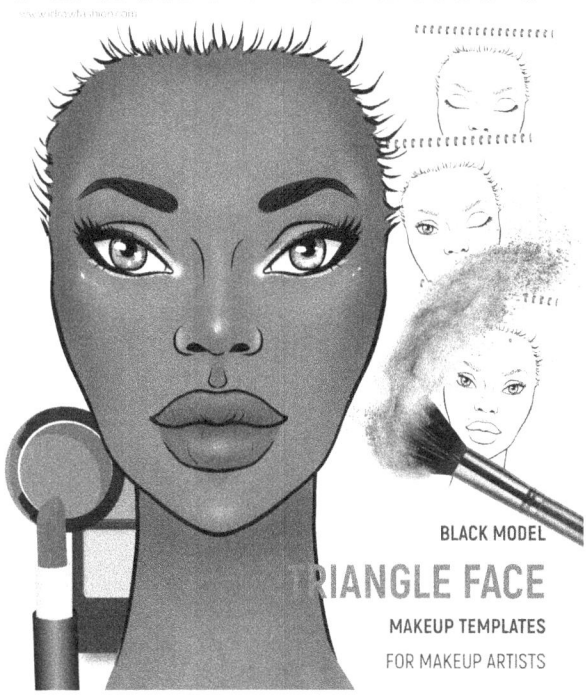